# WORK
# HOW
# YOU ARE
# WIRED

## 12

### Data-Driven Steps to
### Finding a Job You Love

## WILLIAM
## VANDERBLOEMEN

HarperCollins
Leadership

An Imprint of HarperCollins

Work How You Are Wired
© 2025 by William Vanderbloemen

Published by HarperCollins Leadership, an imprint of HarperCollins
Focus LLC, 501 Nelson Place, Nashville, TN 37214, USA.

Any internet addresses, phone numbers, or company or product
information printed in this book are offered as a resource and are not
intended in any way to be or to imply an endorsement by HarperCollins
Leadership, nor does HarperCollins Leadership vouch for the existence,
content, or services of these sites, phone numbers, companies, or
products beyond the life of this book.

ISBN 978-1-4002-5381-4 (ePub)
ISBN 978-1-4002-5380-7 (HC)

HarperCollins Publishers, Macken House, 39/40 Mayor Street Upper,
Dublin 1, D01 C9W8, Ireland (https://www.harpercollins.com)

**Library of Congress Cataloging-in-Publication Data**
Library of Congress Cataloging-in-Publication
application has been submitted.

Art Direction: Ron Huizinga
Cover Design: Faceout Studio, Addie Lutzo
Interior Design: Neuwirth & Associates, Inc.

Printed in the United States of America
25 26 27 28 29 LBC 5 4 3 2 1

*For my seven children: Matthew, Mary, Sarah, Winnie, Will, Emma, and Macy. I have loved watching you all grow up, and hope that some of what we have learned together will help you launch and continue work that matches how you're wired and leaves the world better for it.*

# CONTENTS

# INTRODUCTION

My family and I were in Barcelona recently, and somewhere between the Basílica de la Sagrada Família, the Magic Fountain, and the next round of paella, I noticed something. Most of the dogs we saw were off leash. They knew how to behave without being reminded. They walked, jogged, and trotted happily alongside their owners. They were, as we were, living their best lives.

And then we saw the German shepherd. He was on a leash, which was a good thing for us, the other dogs, and his owner. He was fighting his owner every step of the way, biting the leash and barking in protest of his circumstances.

It struck me: Some dogs are simply more successful at Catalan city life than others. And it's not because some dogs are good and some are bad; it's because asking certain types of animals to behave in a way that goes against their internal wiring is setting up all involved for unhappiness. Would we want a papillon heading the ski patrol team when we're lost in the Alps? Would we ask a Newfoundland to live with us in our Tokyo apartment? We don't use beagles for police work, and we don't rely on Irish wolfhounds to be Seeing Eye dogs. These scenarios don't work for them, and they don't work for us.

It reminds me of the quote "Everybody is a genius. But if you judge a fish by its ability to climb a tree, it will live its whole life believing that it is stupid." We're not all good at the same things.

We don't (generally) ask dogs to do things they're not cut out for, so why should we ask that of ourselves? I don't think we should, and I don't think we have to. I think we can find jobs that work with our own unique dispositions.

## SUCCESS AND HAPPINESS AREN'T NECESSARILY THE SAME

In my last book, *Be the Unicorn*, I wrote about the twelve most important characteristics possessed by successful people (I call them "Unicorns" because they're rare, valuable, and can do amazing things). These twelve attributes, I maintain, are your keys to getting hired and being the best of the best among your competition. Successful people know how to optimize their strongest attributes and work on their weaknesses.

This, I can assure you, will help you find success.

But success in the workplace doesn't always equal happiness. And I have a hunch as to why. There are plenty of bestselling books out there that help us change ourselves for the sake of being more successful at work. Many help introverts find their voice, plenty are aimed at women trying to climb the corporate ladder, and some are as granular as succeeding in a particular field (who knew accounting was such a competition?). The overall message is clear: You have to change. Not necessarily a lot. Maybe you're just a few tiny tweaks away from the sky being the limit on your career. But even so. Some change is required. You won't be successful being yourself. No way. Throw that foolish notion right out the window.

Do we really need to hide who we are in order to be successful? Now, I'm not saying we should go around being unapologetically ourselves. Decorum is required. Social standards must be maintained. If being yourself means being a jerk and wearing a bathrobe in the office, well then, you may want to take a look at the "change your personality" booklist after all.

But I argue that you can be authentically yourself and be successful and, yes, even happy in your work. Because how can you be happy if you're not being yourself?

With this book, I've decided to engage in more rounds of research and hunt for trends once again. I set off to find which "Unicorn" traits led to happiness in particular fields. Not everyone can be a top scorer in all twelve traits, but everyone excels in at least one trait. I was determined to find how playing to your top Unicorn trait leads to significant happiness at work.

## LIVING THE DREAM. OR NOT.

Here's one thing I found early on: Happiness in your career is not about having a "dream job." When my kids were little, it seemed like every boy wanted to be a professional athlete and every girl wanted to be a marine biologist. I think now, what would have happened if they'd all gotten the career of their dreams? Some would be living their best life, sure. But a far bigger majority would be realizing that what looks good on the outside simply isn't what makes them happy.

There are happy doctors and miserable ones. Joyful CEOs and those counting down the days until retirement. And I'm willing to bet we've all had teachers who clearly loved their jobs and at least one who seemed out to make her students as unhappy as she was. My point is, it's not about the job; it's about the person doing the job. If you're not cut out to be a lion tamer in the first place, you're not going to be a happy lion tamer.

The common denominator is that all of the happily employed people I spoke to and researched had figured out who they are and what kind of job would best suit them. They discovered the conditions and factors that made them happy and found a career that aligns with their strengths.

But this is just the tip of the happiness-at-work iceberg. It's all well and good to know that you should find a job that has the right formula for your own personal success and happiness. It's quite another to figure out what that formula is.

That's where data comes in. Remember taking that career test in grade school where you were told you'd make a great federal judge or an exemplary lighthouse keeper? In this book, I've taken that concept and mapped it against hundreds of thousands of data points.

I've surveyed thousands of people in the workforce. I've asked what their job is and how they feel about it. I've also asked them to report their scores on leading personality assessments and share their dominant Unicorn trait from the Vander Index assessment. It's no secret that some people are just better suited to their jobs than others. Now we're going to find out why, and we're going to find out how you can achieve this same success and happiness too.

Let's get started.

# (ALMOST) EVERYONE HATES THEIR JOB

There's a famous scene in *Mad Men* where a frustrated and exhausted Peggy expresses her resentment at not getting more recognition for her successful ideas. As the conversation turns to yelling, Don, crisp of shirt and fresh of cocktail, says, "It's your job. I give you money; you give me ideas."

"And you never say thank you," sniffs Peggy.

"That's what the money is for!" shouts Don.

He goes on: "You're young. You will get your recognition, and honestly, it is absolutely ridiculous to be two years into your career and counting your ideas. Everything to you is an opportunity. And you should be thanking me every morning when you wake up, along with Jesus, for giving you another day."

Don Draper represents one school of thought when it comes to work. Namely, work is work. It's a transaction. And you shouldn't be emotionally attached to your job.

As much as I loved *Mad Men*, I find that this attitude, like so many other aspects of the show, doesn't quite square with modern life.

## PERCENTAGE OF PEOPLE
## WHO HATE THEIR JOB

The stats vary when it comes to the percentage of people who hate their job. I've read reports that have it as high as 70 percent and as low as 39 percent. Anecdotally, there's at least one coffee shop here in Houston where I'm fairly sure 100 percent of those surveyed would report being absolutely miserable. At least that's the impression one gets when trying to order a flat white.

A report from Gallup, "State of the Global Workplace: 2024," found that 62 percent of people were disengaged and emotionally detached at work, and 15 percent described themselves as "miserable."[1]

Most concerning is the number of younger workers who are unhappy. Yes, it takes a while to find one's footing, but the numbers don't look promising for twentysomethings. A Pew Research study done in 2023 found 56 percent of workers under thirty were not satisfied with their jobs. Close behind, 49 percent of people between ages thirty and forty-nine aren't particularly happy either.[2]

Twenty-five is a long way from retirement age. Heck, even forty-nine is far enough out. When you've got that many more years ahead, it's worth taking the time to find work that makes you happy.

### SIX REASONS WHY PEOPLE HATE THEIR JOB

While I've met a few people over the years who didn't seem to need a reason to hate their job, research shows there are some common factors that translate to being unhappy at work.

1. **TOXIC WORK ENVIRONMENT.** Vindictive coworkers, office politics, and unhealthy culture can make even the best job lose its appeal.

2. **BAD MANAGEMENT.** Without a supervisor in your corner, effective communication, or solid faith in leadership, it's difficult to be satisfied at work.

3. **LACK OF WORK-LIFE BALANCE.** When workers are expected to be at the beck and call of their employer, burnout and resentment can occur—and fast.

4. **BAD PAY.** More information than ever is available online on salaries and industry standards. If they're not being compensated properly, employees will, at best, move on or, worse, stay and quiet quit.

5. **LACK OF OPPORTUNITY FOR ADVANCEMENT.** If it looks like their opportunities are limited and that there's no chance of meaningful promotion, employees begin to lose hope.

> **6. LACK OF PURPOSE.** Having a strong sense of why isn't the only way to feel satisfied at work, but it's an important—if not the most important—one.

## WHY YOU SHOULDN'T HAVE TO HATE YOUR JOB

Our careers are requiring more of us than ever. Our parents and grandparents could leave work at work. They didn't have computers, much less cell phones with pinging reminders of work email coming through at all hours. As soon as the office was in the rearview mirror, they could think about other things: hobbies, evening plans, the Manhattan that was waiting for them at home. Forty is a lot of hours, but if those hours stay at work, it's less devastating to spend them unhappily.

If you're going to have to work—and most of us do—you're going to have to like it. Life is far too short to have so much of it dominated by unhappiness or discontent.

## THE TOUGH LOVE OF A FIRST JOB

I'm not saying that every single job we ever have should be all rainbows and butterflies. It's good for us to meet with some adversity at the beginning of our careers. We're supposed to have undesirable jobs when we're starting out. It builds character and makes us all the more grateful for when we get to the place we want to go.

I'm showing my age here, but I got my first job when I was nine. Yep. No one looked too closely at the child labor laws back then.

As my children would say, it was the 1900s. Ancient history. I was a newspaper boy. It was a six-day-a-week job. And, like most first jobs, it was thankless. And, like most first jobs, it was maybe the best job I could have had. I learned so much. I had to keep my own P&Ls. I did sales and collections. I even got into mergers and acquisitions as I bought out a couple of routes from my peers.

In the three and a half years I was a newspaper carrier, my mom helped me once. There was a tornado watch, so she drove me that day. Other than that, neither snow nor rain nor unleashed dogs (because why bother with leash laws?) would keep young William from delivering your paper.

Even in our early experiences, we are learning about ourselves and gaining valuable insight as to what parts of working we love and what parts we'd like to avoid. A friend did groundskeeping at a local liberal arts college during his high school summers. He found he liked the solitude of working in a flower bed or riding a lawn mower through the quad. Solitary work was for him, he learned. But the 6:00 a.m. start time and $4.25 per hour pay rate were not. Now he quite happily works from home, alone, makes a great deal more than minimum wage, and doesn't accept invites for meetings before ten in the morning.

## DEMANDING BETTER

People like to take shots at the younger generations—the youngest millennials and Gen Z—by claiming that they're "soft" or "entitled." But one thing I appreciate about younger people is their idealism and reluctance to settle. Loving your job, being passionate about what you do, and feeling the need to work somewhere that shares your values are concepts that they've brought to the workforce. And I, for one, think they're way overdue.

When so much of the world their adult selves are stepping into isn't what they would have chosen, they're finding the strength to change what they can. The idea of "company culture" was born in the 1980s, but millennials and Gen Z helped make it mainstream.

What we're experiencing now is a sort of "workplace enlightenment," with new demands for workplaces that are, if not contributing to, at least not taking from, one's pursuit of happiness. Enter: culture. Enter: an employer's incentive to maintain a healthy workplace culture.

Seventeenth- and eighteenth-century enlightenment thinkers had the audacity to posit that humans deserve the opportunity to be happy. What's more, they viewed it as a governmental responsibility to protect people's right to be happy. I hope we can agree that we all deserve to be happy. Locke and Rousseau put the onus on government to create conditions that help protect people's right to happiness, and it's an employer's duty to support conditions that support employee happiness.

But this doesn't mean it's an employer's duty to *make* their employees happy. It simply means that they cannot create hostile work environments. When all other basic needs are met, happiness is, ultimately, up to the individual employee. It's up to you.

And that's just who I'm here to help: You and other individuals, each with your own interests and needs and talents, can find your own personal code for workplace happiness.

## CHAPTER 2

# COME ON, GET HAPPY

The recipe for happiness can be complicated or very simple. We're complex creatures, and there's no panacea that guarantees happiness to everyone. One of us might require nothing more than a hot cup of coffee in a silent house in the morning. Others might need a more carefully calibrated combination of factors. To each their own. But I do know this: It's really hard to be happy at work without knowing what makes you happy at work. Sounds a bit tautological, I know. But when we figure out what's going to work for our happiness and what works against it, we're far closer to finding the job that we can love.

Happiness at work does not necessarily mean you're going to be happier in the rest of your life, but it's a key indicator that it will. Likewise, being happy at home can greatly increase your likelihood of being happy at work. I think the two are too intertwined to be pieced out as easily as it was in the *Mad Men* era. Happy at home could mean not having to worry about bills piling up or the well-being of your children or deferred dreams and ambitions. Happy at work could mean making enough money to pay the bills and take care of your children, feeling a sense of purpose and fulfillment in what you do. It's a flywheel of reinforcement.

But whether the happy-at-work chicken or happy-at-home egg comes first, you need and deserve to be happy at work. And everyone deserves for *other* people to be happy at work too.

## HAPPY PEOPLE JUST DON'T SHOOT THEIR HUSBANDS . . . THEY JUST DON'T.

I'm a big believer in exercise and the power of endorphins. So I agree with the famous quote from Reese Witherspoon's character, Elle Woods, in *Legally Blonde*: "Exercise gives you endorphins. Endorphins make you happy. Happy people just don't shoot their husbands . . . they just don't." This is a strong endorsement for exercise, but it's also an opportunity for me to make a case for happiness at work as a matter of public health. It's simply in everyone's best interest for people to be happier.

Consider the countries perennially at the top of the list in the "World Happiness Report." The top spots have been dominated for years now by the Nordic countries, with Finland winning the title of Happiest Country for 2024.[1]

Happy countries are safer. Far fewer mariticides (or any other -cides, for that matter) occur in happy countries than in gloomier places like, I'm sad to report, the United States. Nordic countries have a culture of robust social support systems, lower crime rates, and higher standards of living. When you and your family can count on safety nets and nicer living conditions, as our friends in Denmark, Sweden, Norway, and the rest enjoy, there are a lot fewer reasons to commit crime. So, again, it's circular: Happiness makes you safe or safety makes you happy. Either way, the Nordic countries have bet on happiness, and it's to the benefit of the people who live there.

There's not a lot of downsides when you make happiness a priority. But if relocating to Trondheim isn't in your future, you must do what you can to find happiness where you are.

## WHAT MAKES YOU HAPPY

Happiness, or at least the pursuit of happiness, is having a moment. Big-name colleges like Harvard and UC Berkeley have high-profile classes and graduate programming in the science of happiness. Researchers have studied the facts, stats, and anecdotal evidence to come up with a list of factors that contribute to a person's happiness. Depending on where you look for these factors, you may find more or less, but the main ideas are consistent across all studies.

**SIX FACTORS THAT CONTRIBUTE TO HAPPINESS**

1. **POSITIVE CONNECTIONS.** When you're connected—whether to family, friends, or other aspects of your community—you have built-in emotional support and the feeling that you're in the right place.

2. **BEING THANKFUL.** When you're mindful and have a sense of gratitude for the good things in your life, it encourages a positive mindset.

3. **GOOD HEALTH.** Your health really is your (happiness) wealth. Being in good physical health and maintaining it with nutritious food, exercise, and enough sleep can make all the difference between an unhappy you and a happy you.

4. **RESILIENCE AND PERSPECTIVE.** Being able to cope with life can help you stay happy, or at least at peace, when curveballs are thrown your way. Plus, knowing the difference between tragedy and burned potatoes can obviate the need for resilience in the first place.

5. **LEARNING.** Trying new things, exploring new hobbies and interests helps us feel accomplished and fulfilled.

6. **PURPOSE.** At work, at home, in your community, or all three, when you put effort and time into activities that align with your beliefs and values, you gain a sense of purpose.

Now, let's bring this list home. Or rather, to the office. What contributes to a person's happiness at work?

## SIX KEYS TO BEING HAPPY AT WORK

1. **HAVING A GOOD BOSS.** Knowing your supervisor has your best interests in mind and having a good relationship with them can make an otherwise not-so-great job downright tolerable.

2. **WORK-LIFE BALANCE.** When you're not on the clock 24/7 and you feel like your time is actually your own, you're much more likely to be happy during the time you are at work.

3. **MAKING ENOUGH MONEY.** If your basic needs aren't met in the form of a fair, living wage, you're not going to be happy even if many other happy-at-work boxes are checked.

4. **AUTONOMY AND FLEXIBILITY.** Being treated like a responsible adult who is capable of doing their work without micromanagement is a humane and respectful approach employers can take that will help their employees be happier.

5. **PROFESSIONAL GROWTH.** Having the chance to advance in your career makes a person feel like they've got a future at their job, which makes them more content and confident.

6. **MEANINGFUL WORK.** Purpose. There it is again! Having a sense of purpose and believing in your work is a key component to workplace happiness. In fact, research says that it's the most important workplace happiness factor.[2]

No great shock that the list of why people are happy in their jobs is pretty much the inverse of why people hate their jobs. And it's also no coincidence that there's 50 percent overlap between what makes a person happy in general and what makes a person happy at work. Positive connections, continuous learning, and a sense of purpose are good for your mental health no matter where you are.

## MONEY MATTERS

"Do what you love, and you'll never have to work a day in your life" is a nice sentiment, but in reality, work is work, even if you love it. And you deserve to be paid for it. It's long been taboo, especially at work, to talk about how much you get paid. That has historically served C-suite executives, owners, executive boards, and anyone else interested in keeping costs down for the sake of maximum profit. If no one knows how much the other is making, it's easier to keep salaries low. Now, I'm as big a fan of profit as the next guy, and I certainly don't think people should be paid more than what's fair. Capitalism works, thanks very much. But I'm also against keeping people from being paid what they're worth. In a world of increasingly available salary information (think websites like Glassdoor, SalaryExpert, Salary.com, Indeed, and the Bureau of Labor Statistics), the jig is pretty much up. You'll know if you're not being compensated correctly. In fact, a large part of my company's business is helping organizations be sure they're paying their people correctly.

Paying people fairly is a philosophy that is good not only for employees; it's good for business. Pew Research did a study that found 63 percent of people who left their jobs did so because of bad pay.[3] Replacing good employees is incredibly costly. There's the time spent in finding a replacement, the gap in productivity while training a new person, and it's likely a new hire will require a bigger starting salary than your outgoing worker earned.

Fair pay is important to all sides of the business. And it should be important to you. Anyone who has told you money doesn't buy happiness is either trying to sell you on a wage that's below what you're worth, has never had to choose between food and heating that month, or has never paid well over face value for tickets to the Eras Tour for themselves or their daughter. Money doesn't guarantee happiness, but it sure buys a lot of things that help.

The conventional wisdom, made popular by a 2010 study, was that if you make more than $75,000 a year, more money doesn't make you happier. Once you've reached the $75K threshold, you're as happy as you're going to be. Well, a lot has happened since then. One of the same researchers from the 2010 study, Daniel Kahneman, coauthored a new study in 2023 with lead authors Matthew A. Killingsworth and Barbara Mellers.[4] Their research concluded that, yeah, at this point more money does make you happier. They found that a majority of people reported rising happiness as their salaries increased up to $500,000 a year. From there, the data runs out. So it's possible even more money makes for more happiness in general. But for now, we can stick with the conclusion that, even if it's up to "only" half a million dollars a year, more money increases your likelihood of being happier.

And all this is borne out by the happiness-at-work findings: Salary is a huge contributor to workplace happiness. Don't let anyone tell you money doesn't matter.

## DO YOU HATE YOUR JOB?
## OR DOES YOUR JOB HATE YOU?

It's funny to think of your job actively hating you, like it's some sort of unstoppable monster or insidious parasite, just waiting there, day in, day out, to suck out all your joy and make you as miserable as possible. Okay, maybe it's not laugh-out-loud funny, but still. It's a way to cope when you're absolutely hating your job.

I wrote an article for *Forbes* last year that got above average traction. It obviously struck a chord. In it, I outline what I think is the secret to finding a career that will make you both happy and successful. It's about answering five key questions to determine whether you're going to love a job and if that job will love you back.

1. **Is your job something you're good at?** It's absolutely soul crushing to struggle in a position that you're just not cut out for. The money you might make and the status of a job won't help you if you're not good at it.

2. **Do you enjoy it?** You can be the best at what you do, but if you don't enjoy it, you're not going to be checking much off the list of workplace happiness indicators.

3. **Is this a job that the world needs?** This one is fairly subjective, but if nothing else, it's a really good idea to check the trends to see if you can predict whether your dream job of "landline installer" or "coal mine foreperson" or "beachfront tiki bar owner in Florida" is going to still be an option a decade from now.

4. **Can I make a living doing this job?** Again. Money matters.

5. **Will my work leave the world better than I found it?** Here's where meaningful work and purpose come in.

If you can answer yes to these questions, then you're on the right track. If not, you'll want to keep up the quest for the job that's best for you.

---

### IKIGAI AT WORK

The questions I asked in my *Forbes* article align very well with a new trend: *ikigai*. It's new to us Westerners, I should say. In Japan, it's been around for centuries. *Ikigai* is a Japanese philosophy that helps people identify the things that give their lives meaning and purpose. It's about finding joy and gratitude in simple, everyday things.

A book called *Ikigai: The Japanese Secret to a Long and Happy Life*, by Héctor García and Francesc Miralles, helped put the concept on our Western radars. And now the interpretation of *ikigai* that we use today is career and purpose focused. It's about finding your dream job and living a life with meaning. The four pillars, in this context, of *ikigai* are these questions:

1. What do I love?

2. What does the world need?

---

3. What am I good at?

4. What can I get paid for?

Answer these questions in a Venn diagram, and where they overlap is where you'll find your *ikigai*.

## THIS ABOVE ALL, TO THINE OWN SELF BE TRUE

Good advice can come from anyone, even guys who make every wrong decision and ultimately get stabbed to death while hiding behind a tapestry. Polonius in *Hamlet* was, for better or worse, true to himself, and so was the recipient of his wisdom, his son, Laertes. And although it didn't really work out for either of them, it's still good advice. I promise.

Career success and happiness hinges on knowing yourself and letting that knowledge guide your decisions. I've often said that while I *can* do detail-oriented work, and I *can* do routine work, it drains me like nothing else. I am happiest and most successful when I have new tasks thrown at me nearly every day. That makes me an ideal candidate for a field like marketing, sales, client relations, and other dynamic, unpredictable jobs. It also proves to me that I would be a horrible accountant or compliance officer or any job that asks for the same task to be done over and over, day in, day out.

In that same *Forbes* article, I wrote about the world-famous heart surgeon and Houstonian Denton Cooley. He was a titan in his field and changed the industry. Certainly he was a person to emulate. But reading more about him, I discovered that a claim to fame and a reason for his success was that he performed the same surgery more than a hundred thousand times. Great for him! Great for the world! Not great for someone like me. That kind of job would make me crazy, and I probably wouldn't be very good at it. Heart patients the world over can be glad I didn't follow Dr. Cooley's path.

## WHEN YOUR JOB IS YOUR VOCATION

There's a quote I love by Frederick Buechner. He wrote, "The place God calls you to is the place where your deep gladness and the world's deep hunger meet." If you're not religious, you can swap "your vocation" for "the place God calls you." It's the idea that where you will fit in and find the most fulfillment is where the thing that makes you happy is also a service the world needs. We can get as aspirational as you'd like here: teachers inspiring the next generation to do great things. Men and women rushing into burning buildings to save lives. Diplomats and heads of state negotiating peace. Kindhearted people creating sanctuary for abused and abandoned animals. Chefs who feed the homeless. Public defenders who protect the innocent when no one else will. It makes you feel good, doesn't it?

We should all be so lucky as to experience this kind of work. A vocation is the ideal, perhaps, a fulfillment of a deep need and purpose and contributing to the world. It checks so many of the happiness-in-work and happiness-in-life boxes. But it doesn't have to be the goal. You can be happy without a vocation.

## YOUR PASSION AND PURPOSE ARE IMPORTANT—BUT THEY MIGHT NOT HAVE ANYTHING TO DO WITH YOUR JOB

Following your purpose and "deep gladness" can help you discover the job where you'll be happiest and most successful, but here's the thing: Your job might not actually have that much to do with your sense of purpose at all. You can be perfectly happy, content, and feel 100 percent true to yourself in a job that's just a job. You can find your life's work outside of work. Your job doesn't have to be what makes you you.

. This is a relatively new concept, at least here in the United States. It always struck me when, prepandemic, we used to travel to Europe: No one asked about what my wife or I did for a living. This staple of American small talk, "What do you do for work?" didn't exist there. Our identity wasn't tied to our work. It was a little destabilizing, to be honest. What were we if not our professions? They'd ask about where we lived, our thoughts on US politics, where else we'd traveled. What we did for a living didn't come up. It was a real *Emily in Paris*–style bit of culture shock.

In the United States, career and identity are so intertwined that "main character gets fired" has become a staple of sitcom plots. Our beloved protagonists become unhinged when they no longer have a job they can tie their identity to. They don't know who they are anymore. Michael Scott in *The Office*, Chandler Bing in *Friends*, Jessica Day in *New Girl*, and even Don Draper in *Mad Men* all experience this. In television, as so often in life, being fired at first leads to instability, confusion, and erratic behavior. But then our heroes experience introspection, positive change, and are ultimately better off for the upheaval.

I think for a lot of people, the pandemic helped drive a wedge between our jobs and our identities in a similar way. If you no longer went into the office in the morning, freshly showered, in tailored suits with carefully coiffed hair, ready to take on the day starting with your Monday morning all-staff meeting in the conference room, who were you? The same work, in many cases, could be done from home. But without all the trappings of "career," without office politics and lunch orders and Debbie's leftover birthday cake in the kitchen, who were we?

Enter: the era of everyone making sourdough bread. I think a lot of us replaced who we were at the office with a new version of ourselves that would be "who we were at home." We'd never really thought about that person before. We never really had time. But if there's one good thing the pandemic brought us, it was time. Suddenly, we had to reconcile our office selves and our at-home selves. For some of us, it was a struggle. For some, it was a gift.

Some of us found out that our job wasn't everything. We found that our passions and purpose were found elsewhere. Your job should make you happy, but it doesn't have to be who you are. You don't have to make it, as the youth say, your whole identity. You might be happy to have a job you don't hate, earn the paycheck, and then focus on the things that actually do make you happy—your sourdough starters, your music, your painting or travel or volunteer work or anything else that is separate from the person who earns the salary.

## A CHANCE FOR EXALTATION

There's a famous quote by President Jimmy Carter: "In all of our lives, there are usually a few precious moments when we feel exalted—that is, when we reach above our normal level of existence to a higher plane of excitement and achievement . . . I predict that every one of you who volunteers to help others in need will feel this same sense of exaltation. I believe that, in making what seems to be a sacrifice, you will find fulfillment in the memorable experience of helping others less fortunate than yourself."

President Carter, by all accounts, was happy in his job. He was a man of great integrity and did the right thing for people even when it hurt him politically. But I think you could argue that he got greater happiness from helping others, outside of his job. He lived by the demands of his faith, which were, as he put it, "That I do whatever I can, wherever I am, whenever I can, for as long as I can with whatever I have to try to make a difference."

He made all the difference to suffering people all across the world, and I hope he's resting happily knowing how much good he did.

## EITHER WAY WORKS

My point is: Whether your identity and happiness are tied to your job or your job is just a paycheck, you can be happy. Shoot for finding your vocation. Dream big. Do everything you can to find what you were meant to do and what the world needs. You deserve a job that gives you purpose and happiness. That's my goal for you. But if you fall short of that in your career, you can still be just as happy in a job that is more transactional, as long as that job works for you.

# CHAPTER 3

# THE METHODOLOGY

*I have this theory that if you don't love your job,
you don't have a chance in hell of being good at it*

— Sylvie Grateau, *Emily in Paris*

We know what makes people happy. Now we need to know what makes you happy and how to apply it to your career. For this, as in a lot of things, I turn to the data. We surveyed thousands of working people to discover:

- How happy they were at work—we learned as much from the very unhappy people as we did from the happy ones
- Their Enneagram, Vander Index, and DiSC personality test scores
- Where their personality caused points of friction or flow at work; which traits caused them to be especially happy or particularly miserable

- How long they've been in a particular field
- Their favorite subjects in school
- What their ideal job looks like

Using all these data points, we sliced, diced, and found some pretty clear trends that helped us identify which jobs worked best for each of the twelve Unicorn traits we discovered in *Be the Unicorn*. The traits are fast, authentic, agile, solver, anticipator, prepared, self-aware, curious, connected, likable, productive, and purpose-driven. Knowing where you excel among the twelve traits helps you better understand the circumstances under which you might be happiest.

## THIS ISN'T A PERSONALITY ASSESSMENT

What we're doing here is trying to find the best pieces of information that can help you make the best career decisions. In my opinion, no one does personality assessments, especially as they relate to the workplace, better than Enneagram and DiSC. They are both so rich in research, psychology, and theory that I'm not going to try to improve upon them. But I, too, aspire to be happy at work, so I did what brings me joy: I used these assessments along with other data points in my quest to find the most meaningful information for people looking for workplace happiness.

You will be better served by this book if you're starting with the same data about yourself that we've collected from thousands of others. Do you know your Enneagram and DiSC results? Have you taken the Vander Index and found your strengths? If you haven't, I suggest you take a moment to collect the data on yourself. From this point on, I invite you to read straight through or flip through the pages and find which sections resonate with you. This book is about helping you be happier, after all, and I'm not the boss of you. Read it however you choose and enjoy learning more about yourself and which circumstances could make you happier in your job.

# CHAPTER 4

# SWIFT SUCCESS
## FINDING HAPPINESS AS THE FAST

Speed is not a luxury; it's a necessity.

—Oscar de la Renta

Speed is the cornerstone of prosperity.

—John Paul Getty

Speed wins. We know that. And yet for so many of us, we spend precious time waiting. We wait to respond to a text, we wait to get the answer exactly right, or we just can't be bothered to deal with the topic at hand. Paralysis by analysis or being overwhelmed by other aspects of life stop too many otherwise solid leaders and bright thinkers in their paths. But this isn't so for the Fast, the first trait tackled in *Be the Unicorn*. The Fast have response time and balance between perfect and good enough all figured out. And they use their skills to great advantage over their completion.

You might be part of the Fast crowd if:

- You're the first to respond in group texts.
- You're an Enneagram type 3 (18 percent of the Fast are).
- You're a high D, like 30 percent of the Fast, or high i (29 percent) DiSC assessment.
- Productive (24 percent) and Connected (22 percent) are your next highest Vander Index traits.
- Curious is your weakest Vander Index trait (only 7 percent of the Fast rank above average for Curious).
- The next hot piece of technology or trendy new clothing item is already on its way to you by the time your friends have even heard of it.
- You've been told by teachers or supervisors to "take your time" more.
- Math is your favorite subject (19 percent of the Fast would describe themselves as "mathletes").
- You get impatient with more methodical thinkers.
- You've got a full schedule from sunup to sundown, and you wouldn't change a thing about it.

## MICRO TRAITS OF THE FAST

Nothing gets past the Fast. Noticing things others don't is part of what makes them successful and happy. The Fast Unicorns share two essential traits.

- **Attentive.** Pilot Rory M. says, "There's a Jack Welch quote I love. It goes, 'Attention to detail is critical when it comes to delivering high-quality work. Being attentive ensures that nothing slips through the cracks and that you can identify potential issues before they become significant problems.' Paying attention has helped me excel in all aspects of my life, and it's helped me build trust and credibility with my team."

- **Decisive.** Embracing decisiveness and avoiding second-guessing oneself is just as vital to the Fast. Gamer Garrit L. says, "I have to trust my instincts and make fast decisions. It's almost unconscious at this point. By trusting your instincts and making prompt decisions, you demonstrate confidence, which is essential for me."

### THE HAPPIEST FAST PERSON YOU KNOW:
### HULDAH GRONVALL

"I was faster earlier in my career when I didn't have so many emails," quips Huldah Gronvall.

But in spite of increased workload and responsibilities—and what she might say—Gronvall remains on top of things, as quick and nimble as she ever was.

Gronvall is the director of construction for an athletic company and lives in a Minneapolis suburb. It's her job to make sure company facilities nationwide are kept as in shape as the people using them. She deploys her team the instant a need arises.

"You have to be fast," she says. "Things happen without any notice. There are members that use the clubs and we need to make sure they're safe. A tile falls, a treadmill starts on fire, the pool leaks. The first call is sometimes to 9-1-1; the second is to me."

Gronvall loves her job. "It's construction and it's fitness. It's perfect for me," she says.

As far as her career goes, Gronvall acknowledges that being fast didn't have too much to do with where she ended up. It was more like inertia.

"You have a good teacher in one subject, so you follow that and become good at it. Initially that was math for me. I could have done a lot of different things," she says. "But when you're under a certain age, you don't have a lot of agency."

And as it happens, Gronvall had even less agency than most children.

## Math matters

Gronvall was homeschooled in Mankato, Minnesota, until sixth grade.

"When I joined public school, I tested way above in math," she says. "So, yes, I had to learn all of the social skills, but none of the math skills." She laughs. "I had the math skills."

As she excelled in school and in math in particular, Gronvall began to think about what was next and what she could do within the strict confines of her limited options.

Then living in Green Bay, Wisconsin, Gronvall graduated high school and started attending the University of
Wisconsin—Green Bay. "Math turned out to be too theo-
retical for me, so I majored in mathematical physics, which
wasn't a major that they had. So I did independent study,"
she says.

"I was going to go to grad school for physics, but then
realized I'd be in my thirties before making a dollar," she says.
"So, after getting accepted to a bunch of grad schools for
physics, I thought, *How can I apply this differently?* and looked
at structural engineering."

Gronvall started taking "a bunch of construction management electives" and had a revelation: "Construction management is the same work I'd been doing since I was fifteen. It
was the same thing I did at the compound as a cult girl."

**Yes, "cult girl"**
When she was a junior in high school, Gronvall's parents
dropped her off at the main compound of the cult they'd
been part of for Gronvall's whole life. There, she would be
under the direct supervision of the cult leader who, they
hoped, could tame their rebellious girl.

"At no point was I happy to be there or in agreement
with anything they were doing there," she says. Gronvall was
forced to wear long skirts and button-down shirts. At school

no one knew that she lived in a compound forty miles away with five other girls rather than at the nearby address the cult leader had used to get her into the Green Bay school system. One day she came to school with her waist-length hair completely gone. Her head had been shaved because she'd talked back to the leader. No one at school said anything.

"Rapid responsiveness is essential to my success in my career," she says. "But having a quick answer for everything wasn't always in my best interest. Not back then."

**Gaining speed and strength**

As she grew older, Gronvall began to push the boundaries of cult rules and create as normal a life as she could for herself. While enrolled at UWGB (the only place she was allowed to go; this way she could continue to live closely monitored at the compound), she discovered fitness and Ultimate Frisbee.

"There was this guy I had a huge crush on in my linear algebra class," she says. "He and I would go disc golfing and then he introduced me to Ultimate Frisbee." From there, Gronvall started experiencing a bit more of typical college life. She secretly bought clothes for sports and working out. She was confident none of the other cult kids would ever step foot in the gym and discover her. They weren't allowed to and, unlike Gronvall, weren't brave enough to try.

"Turns out the guy didn't have a crush back on the weird cult girl," she says. "But I got really into fitness. And I got really strong."

As Gronvall's physical strength increased, so did her "brazen indifference" at the compound. "People were blown away," she says. "My disrespect wasn't fueled by hope that anything was going to get better or anything. It was more like, 'What do I have to lose?' My future self probably would have begged my past self not to be quite so outspoken."

It was in the spirit of 'what do I have to lose' that Gronvall, during her junior year of college, told the cult leader she was transferring to the University of Wisconsin—Madison and that she would not be coming back. She left out the front door and never looked back. No one pursued her, though she could no longer talk to her family. They were still in the cult and forbidden from speaking to her.

**Life after**

At Madison, Gronvall was off and running. Literally. She joined one of the nation's best Ultimate Frisbee teams. "It's where I really learned how to play," she says. And yes, speed wins in Ultimate Frisbee. "There's a lot of running, sprinting, and making quick decisions. Lots of pivoting and dodging, which is basically what I've done throughout my life to be successful and survive," says Gronvall.

Gronvall graduated, got married, and moved to Washington, DC. She began doing the work to heal from her upbringing and found that exercise was a key component. In DC, she remained an avid Ultimate Frisbee player, but after her first daughter was born, she "got really into CrossFit.

"A friend was into it—it was just coming on the market," she says. "And you know the most annoying part about people who do CrossFit: They don't shut up about CrossFit. I knew how to lift by what I'd taught myself at the college gym, and CrossFit took it from there."

A recruiter found her and Gronvall began working for her current company. "It's ideal," she says. "I'm in control, I have a team I love and trust, and I can use my responsiveness for everyone's benefit."

Gronvall says that speed isn't required of her at work. "It's expected." She goes on: "It's imperative to be responsive and act quickly. If you couldn't do that, you wouldn't do this job. But I can and I do, and I couldn't be happier."

## WHAT HAPPINESS LOOKS LIKE
## AT WORK WHEN YOU'RE FAST

One of the key elements that contribute to the happiness of our Fast Unicorns is the ability to stay constantly engaged. They thrive in environments that demand quick decision-making and high levels of attentiveness. Fast thinkers often find joy in tackling challenges head-on and in swiftly overcoming obstacles.

Another factor that plays a significant role in Fast Unicorn job satisfaction is the sense of accomplishment that comes from making prompt decisions and seeing immediate results. The ability to trust their instincts and make confident choices is a source of pride and motivation for them. This decisiveness not only boosts their self-esteem but also garners respect from their colleagues and superiors. It reminds me of the famous scene in *Raiders of the Lost Ark* where a crowd in a bustling marketplace suddenly parts and Indy is faced with a sword-wielding adversary. The music intensifies and the swordsman makes threatening flourishes with his blade. We brace ourselves for an epic fight.

And then Indy just takes out his gun and shoots the guy.

The Fast don't necessarily advocate violence, but they do support any approach that gets the job done faster and more efficiently. Even if it may not look as cool. Indy made a quick decision, and it worked.

Careers where the Fast work best:

- Stockbroker
- ER/trauma surgeon
- Track star
- Emergency vet
- Police officer
- Gamer

- Auctioneer
- House flipper / Realtor
- Personal assistant
- Executive assistant
- Trial lawyer
- Crisis response
- Television producer
- Triage nurse
- Emergency medical technician (EMT)
- Water ski team member
- Jamaican bobsled team member
- Professor/archaeologist turned protector of antiquities

As we will see with all our types, the Fast thrive when the six workplace happiness factors are met for them.

### Having a good boss

Leadership is particularly important for fast thinkers. At best, a good boss provides the necessary guidance and support, enabling fast thinkers to excel in their roles. At worst, they have the good sense to get out of the way of their Fast Unicorn. As Celia D., a vet tech, put it, "Having a boss who understands my need for speed and efficiency makes all the difference. They trust me to make quick decisions and they support me in them."

### Work-life balance

For the Fast, it's less of a balance and more of a blend. Maintaining a work-life balance is less about strict separation and more about finding an effective blend between professional and personal pursuits. After all, they don't turn off their "fast"-ness when they leave the office. The Fast thrive in environments where they can integrate their rapid problem-solving skills and quick decision-making abilities whether it's at the Tuesday department head meeting or Thursday night volleyball.

"One thing that works for me," says executive assistant Pat S., "is focusing on high-impact activities. By streamlining my schedule and minimizing unnecessary delays, I make sure I can get the most out of my time. And when I can get eight hours of work done in four hours, well, that's just more time to pursue other things that make me happy."

## Making enough money

The Fast seek opportunities to make enough money and then some. These are the "hustlers" of our Unicorns, so don't be surprised when you someday discover their lucrative freelance career.

Like it or not, side hustles are here to stay. And, according to a *Harvard Business Review* study, a full 45 percent of those surveyed said they do side jobs because of the extra financial security it offers them.[1] Perhaps if the Fast were making enough money in the first place, they wouldn't seek other opportunities. But it's also possible that they'd be out there looking for the next thing to do simply because they like the sense of accomplishment.

Jordan M. is a police officer who takes on security work on the side. He says, "My supervisors know about it and are often the ones telling me about opportunities. They know we don't get paid a whole lot here."

## *Autonomy and flexibility*

The Fast recognize the importance of flexibility and seek roles that offer autonomy and the ability to manage their own time. This allows them to adjust their work hours to accommodate personal commitments and avoid burnout.

"I need to get up from my desk and recharge a few times a day," says Karin R., a legal aid. "Whether it's a quick walk outside, a short meditation session, or a few laps around the halls, it helps me to keep my speed and efficiency up."

## *Professional growth*

Having the opportunity to continuously learn and adapt is crucial for the happiness of our Fast Unicorns. They enjoy environments that encourage innovation and provide opportunities for growth and development. Being able to explore new ideas, experiment with different approaches, and stay ahead of the curve keeps them motivated and engaged in their work.

"I'll always jump at the chance to learn something that will make me better and faster at my job," says Ketih, a house flipper. "Speed is just as important as anything else in my line of work, so whatever edge I can get on the competition, I'm there."

## *Meaningful work*

The Fast get all their to-dos done, respond to emails and texts, and will have the grocery shopping done before you set foot in the store, but don't mistake this for a quantity over quality thing. The work they do has to be meaningful, just as it should be for all our worker types.

Says public defender Hannah H., "I like that I'm fast on my feet and can pivot in a heartbeat, but it's all in aid of helping others, and that makes all the difference in me being good at my job versus me loving my job."

---

"Keep it under sixty-five.
We don't wanna get pulled over."

---

## WHERE THE FAST GET STUCK

Because of their efficiency and adaptability, the Fast often find themselves frustrated by certain workplace dynamics that others cope just fine with.

### Pushing molasses up a sandy hill

One common source of frustration that we've heard from our Fast Unicorns is the need to wait for others to catch up. When decisions are delayed, or when team members are slow to respond, the Fast lose patience.

"I can't stand it when I have to sit and wait for others to finish what I completed hours ago," shares Jamie T., who works in sales. "I don't know why we need to accommodate the worst of the talent here."

Our Fast Unicorns also reported being fairly miserable in conditions with excessive bureaucracy and red tape. The need for constant approvals and adherence to rigid protocols can stifle their natural agility and hinder their progress. This can lead to a sense of being bogged down by unnecessary obstacles.

"I get really frustrated when I have to jump through hoops just to get something simple done," says marketing specialist Dana L. "I thrive in environments where I can take immediate action without having to ask for permission at every step."

## Communication, or lack thereof

Workplace environments that lack clear priorities are a constant source of irritation for the Fast. They prefer to have a focused direction and a clear set of goals to aim for. When priorities are constantly shifting, it can lead to confusion and inefficiency—two of the Fast's least favorite things.

"I need to know what the endgame is," explains project manager Allen K. "Without a clear target, it feels like I'm sprinting in all directions without really getting anywhere."

---

**THE HAPPY-AT-WORK CHECKLIST**

If you're a Fast person yourself, it can feel like you're surrounded by people who just drank a bottle of nighttime cough syrup. If you manage a Fast person, it can feel like you're constantly trying to wrangle their energy and action. Here are tips for managing a Fast person.

**Guard against being overcommitted.** Balancing workload is key. Often the Fast can take on more than others, but they shouldn't be overworked either. Help by making sure they feel challenged but not overworked.

---

**When to slow down.** Know when and what they need to slow down on or think through more thoroughly, and when they need to be more intentional; help them in that space.

**Watch which types of meetings work.** Sometimes the think-tank, brainstorm-type of meeting can be the worst thing to happen to the Fast. They want a decision, not talking about possibilities for an hour or more. Make sure they know meetings like that are coming and how they can contribute most effectively.

**Make sure the Fast know they are trusted and know the boundaries/fences that they're able to run in.** An easy way to paralyze or frustrate the Fast is to make them ask for permission on every single detail of a project or task. Give them places to run free and places where they need approval, and then let them run.

**Know how fast to grow.** The Fast want to grow fast. Sometimes that's possible, and sometimes it's not. If they desire growth and an upward trajectory, make sure they can always see how they are making progress or movement toward something, even if their title or role hasn't changed.

**Have general standards of communication across the team.** If you have a Fast person on your team, you want them to be able to embrace being Fast, and you want them to know what to expect from others who aren't as fast. For example, say policy is to respond to emails within twenty-four hours. The Fast will respond in five minutes. The Prepared, another of our Unicorn traits, might take a few hours to think about it. Both are within the guidelines, but you need to help each person be who they are and still work well together, not comparing or expecting unfair things from each other.

**Help them see farther into the future than others.** Let them know the plan for right now and where you're heading if you can. They'll run faster toward their work right now and in the future if you can communicate clearly what you're doing and how it's leading to something down the road.

## JOBS THAT DO NOT WORK FOR THE FAST

If you're Fast, you need a job with a supportive team that recognizes and rewards you. Maybe not all the time, but some of the time. It's not too much to ask. And you need a work culture that values efficiency and speed. Jobs where the sales cycle is fast, where the results are instantaneous, and where there isn't bureaucracy to make you feel like Jack clinging to that door after the ship went down.

Avoid these jobs for your own good and for the good of those you might have had to work with:

- Elder care
- Instructor/teacher
- Horticulture

- Long-term research
- Artist
- Actuary
- University administration
- DMV worker
- Olympic committee member
- Any position where you're in charge of toddlers who insist on putting on their own shoes

## THINGS TO DO RIGHT NOW TO BE HAPPIER

If you're already in the workforce and you find yourself in a job that simply doesn't work for you or you're frustrated to be unemployed, don't despair. It will get better. Probably not as fast as you'd like it to, but then, few things ever happen as fast as you'd like them to.

Here's my advice for bolstering your distress tolerance in the meantime.

### Slow down

I know. You might hate it at first, but I promise if you give yoga or Pilates classes a chance, you'll feel a lot better, mentally and physically. The same goes for meditation. Don't worry, even a few minutes of meditation makes a difference.[2]

If that's too far, try doing a really hard puzzle. Your brain will appreciate the chance to process things a little more slowly.

### Speed up

Good for you for trying something out of your comfort zone in the form of slower, more methodical activities. If that didn't work, lean into the speed you know and love. Take a kickboxing class, go trap shooting, or just lace up your sneakers and run out the door.

*Garden*

I wouldn't recommend this for a career, but nurturing living things, getting your hands dirty, spending time outdoors, and (eventually) reaping the harvest are all very good for your mental health and overall happiness.[3] And if it turns out you tried it and really can't stand gardening, take a moment to find joy in never having to do it again.

## FULL SPEED AHEAD

You're Fast. You know what you value in a job, and you know what won't work for you. Seek out opportunities, try lots of things, but cut and run if it's not for you. The sooner you stop giving your time to causes underserving of it, the faster you'll find your true career happiness. As Sanka Coffie, in one of history's best speed-based sports movies, says, "Cool runnings!"[4]

## TAKEAWAYS

- Look for jobs that require quick decision-making and high levels of attentiveness.
- Avoid any jobs with even a whiff of bureaucracy or slow-moving gears.
- The title of "Zen master" may never be in your future, but some brief and occasional slowing down will do you good.

# CHAPTER 5

# GETTING REAL

## FINDING HAPPINESS AS AN AUTHENTIC PERSON

The privilege of a lifetime is to become who you truly are.

—Carl Jung

We ain't running a chocolate factory or Deutsche Bank.
We got nothing to hide from y'all.

—Ted Lasso

If you've ever signed up for a fun run, given money to a new cause, or overcommitted yourself to a volunteer opportunity, you may have done so because an Authentic person asked you. If you're an Authentic person yourself, you know you have an uncanny ability to connect with people in a way that can completely disarm them. You might be Authentic if:

- You're an Enneagram type 6 (12 percent) or 2 (10 percent), or any of the others because the Authentic people surveyed were pretty evenly distributed among Enneagram types.
- You're a high i (36 percent of Authentic) or S (26 percent) on the DiSC assessment scale.
- Your next top Vander Index traits are Purpose-Driven (33 percent had this as their number two) and Productive (28 percent of the Authentic had this for their next strongest trait).
- You may not be overly burdened with speed, since Fast might be your weakest Vander Index trait (only 8 percent had Fast as a strength).
- What's in fashion doesn't matter to you; you've had your own style since you were five.
- You love history, like 26 percent of your fellow Authentic people.
- You may have been called "a big personality" and "a lot" at some point in your life, but only by boring people.

## MICRO TRAITS OF THE AUTHENTIC

Not all Authentic people are happy. I'm sure you've met some unapologetically "authentic" people who are quire miserable humans. But the Unicorns we've studied who are strongest in authenticity and are happy at work share three micro traits.

- **Honesty.** Authentic Unicorns know they're not always going to make people happy. Their honesty can sometimes be off-putting. But the happiest Unicorns know how to be honest and kind at the same time. Says data administrator

Kay P., "A lady I worked with for many years has said to others, 'If you want someone to help you, go to Kay. What you hear may be hard to hear, but it will be honest and truthful and will help you if you follow her advice. She loves people even though she is blunt and honest, and her heart will show as you get to know her.' It's one of the greatest things someone has said about me, and it's true."

- **Originality.** Most of our happiest Authentic Unicorns initially struggled with their authenticity, but the successful ones have learned to embrace it. Says Liz L., a COO, "I have been pushing the limits on what is possible in my life. I was afraid of public speaking for a while. I didn't even naturally go after roles of leadership. But eventually I learned to ruthlessly show up as myself in everything I do, and it's been very rewarding."

- **Transparency.** When people see that you don't cover up mistakes or hide from your flaws, you'll go further. Production manager Omi D. says this has helped him in his career: "Having worked for various corporations, I've learned authenticity plays a very important role. Being authentic covers a multitude of relationship-related work and helps build relational capital fast. No pretenses, just being real. In the work journey, being authentic offered me an opportunity to improve relationships, work, networking, and communication. Being authentic makes it a lot easier to face challenges along the way. Decision-making is also made easy when you're operating from a place of authenticity."

## THE HAPPIEST AUTHENTIC PERSON YOU KNOW: DAKOTA WHITE

Growing up in Raddison, Wisconsin, Dakota White didn't want to be a skateboarder when he grew up. He already was one. For nearly as long as White's been on Earth, he's been on a skateboard.

White is a professional skateboarder, specializing in transition (as opposed to street) skating. Think: aerial tricks on vert ramps, bowls, and half-pipes—all the really cool moves that come to mind with skateboarding, all the skills that look terrifying, impossible, and a ton of fun.

"My dad had skateboarding and snowboarding chops," says White. "He loved these things, so he wanted to share them with me. When I was a year and five months, they put me on a snowboard. I was like a Weeble. I didn't fall over. Then, when the snow melted, they put me on a skateboard. It was fun, and I loved it."

By age four, White was skilled at both skate- and snowboarding. It was around that time that he decided to focus on skateboarding. He communicated this as eloquently and authentically as any four-year-old could by voicing his displeasure at having cold hands, cold feet, and being outside in the cold.

"I was like, no," he says. "So my dad said, 'Okay, let's skateboard.'"

White went to his first competition and got third place. He was four years old. "The next closest in age was a kid who was thirteen," he says. "I did great, but I also had a blast. My dad realized that maybe there was something there. And from that point on, he drove me every single weekend to Minneapolis."

It was a three-hour drive, but Minneapolis had the closest indoor skate park where White could skate year-round. There, White was finally surrounded by other kids like him, and he started to make friends he still has to this day.

## Sacrifices

White's love for skateboarding never flagged, but his interest in giving up his social life sometimes did.

"I was invited to a classmate's birthday party in first grade, and everyone was going. I wanted to go, but my dad said, 'You're not going to be friends with this kid when you're older, but you will be with the kids at the skate park.' I wasn't happy, but he was right," says White.

"Some of the other parents at the skate park looked at my dad like he was crazy," he says, but White knew his dad knew when to push him and when to let up. Like most parents, White's dad knew the difference between sincere distress and performance.

Between his dad's coaching and White's mindset, he says he learned resilience, how to be true to himself, and a way of approaching challenges that has served him all his life.

"You fall, you dust yourself off, and you try again," he says. "It's a state of mind. I remember breaking my foot trying a new trick. I stayed and landed the trick and then I drove myself to the hospital. Skateboarders are a different breed for sure."

**Turning pro**

The time and effort White and his family put into his skateboarding career began paying off. By six he was a sponsored skater, meaning skate equipment companies would send him products to use and promote. By thirteen, he'd turned pro.

"My dad wanted me to have the best shot at success. He said you never know who's watching and what opportunities I might miss if I didn't present my best self," says White. "He was always careful to get me white Gatorade, not blue, so I wouldn't get stained lips and look like a little kid."

But even with high expectations, White was thriving. Skateboarding, as so many before him have found out, is more than a hobby or a sport. He loved the community, the confidence he gained, and the satisfaction that comes with achieving new skills.

"'Professional skateboarder' sounds like one of the coolest jobs ever," says White. "And it is. I get to travel. I get to skate with people I looked up to as a kid. But turning pro isn't like, 'Okay, I've made it. I can relax.' Turning pro is the beginning of work. There are strict filming schedules. You have to do so many events per year. I'm grateful to be able to do this, but when you're doing what you're passionate about for a job, you have to watch for burnout. It can suck the joy out of the thing you love most if you're not careful."

Unlike other professional sports, there isn't room at the top for a lot of professional skateboarders to make a living solely from being a professional skateboarder. White says that maybe twenty-five skateboarders in the world can be a pro and not have to have other sources of income. There are only so many energy drink and shoe sponsorship deals to go around.

"There's guys that were on the cover of *Thrasher* and work at Home Depot," he says. But the nature of skateboarding and skateboarders is, generally, that it's not about the money or the fame. It's about being your authentic self and doing what you love when you can for as long as you can.

"I've gotten to meet my best friends; I've had opportunities that a lot of people from where I grew up didn't have. But the other thing that skateboarding is, outside of it being a career, it's an artistic coping mechanism for me. If I'm sad, it's what I do. If I'm happy, it's what I do," says White. "I don't need to be a professional to get the joy and mental and physical benefits from it."

**Transition**

White supplements his pro skater income by coaching, teaching camps and clinics, and running skate competitions. For a while he ran a skate park, but it was difficult to maintain his love of skateboarding, much less share it with the next generation, when he was also expected to put in eighty-hour weeks and handle payroll, inventory, and development. Nonprofit skate park boards, he found, don't necessarily share the same values as skaters.

White works with a lot of young skaters, and while he would never discourage anyone from wanting to be a pro skateboarder, he likes to highlight all the possibilities that are available when you make a career out of doing something you love.

"One of the most important things for me to teach kids is that if you are truly passionate about something, there is a way to make it your career. Find the thing that fires you up. If you love skateboarding, there are more options than just being a professional skateboarder. You can make a living being a content creator, doing reviews of new products. If you like art, design boards and logos. If you're good at marketing, do marketing for one of the big brands," says White.

For White, balancing his passion for skateboarding with the necessity to commodify it will always be a challenge, but, he says, "I'm always going to skate. That's who I am as a person. That's what I'll continue to do till my old age. You always want to get better, no matter what your level is. You always want to push your limits. I'm going to skate as long as my body will let me and as long as I'm still finding joy in it."

As of now, White is back home in northern Wisconsin, with his wife, Ali, his four Siberian huskies, and plenty of land and space to "just skate, with no expectations." What he does with the rest of his pro career remains to be seen, but he knows he and his family will be just fine.

"Every skater knows that no matter how bad the fall is, you get up and take one more," he says. "You never leave on a fall."

## WHAT HAPPINESS AT WORK LOOKS LIKE FOR YOU IF YOU'RE AUTHENTIC

The Authentic thrive when their energy and integrity is matched, or at least appreciated, by their coworkers. They like having goals to meet and bring a can-do attitude that rivals that of the plucky kids in old movies where they put on a show and use the old barn as a stage. I'm dating myself here, I know. Jump forward a few decades from Andy Rooney and Judy Garland and think of that Gen X treasure *The Goonies.* Our heroes follow Mikey not because he's cool and knows it all, but because he's sincere, true of heart, and an inspiring speaker. Put that in your bucket, Troy.

The Authentic are the emotional support dogs of our worker types. Because they're so in tune with who they are, they can tell when someone is struggling, and they know just what to do. Whether it's a Cavalier King Charles spaniel snuggling on a lap for as many hours as it takes or a corgi running up with a ball and a wiggle of their generous backside, authentic people know the secret to motivating others and finding joy in their everyday lives. That is, if they use their authenticity for good. As I mentioned in my previous Unicorn book, the Authentic, when not happy, have the tendency to use "just being authentic" as an excuse for not being their best selves. But authentic people who are happy and in the right place know how to temper their honesty with kindness.

You've never felt a strong urge to fit in, if you're authentic. You're an individualist through and through. You can cry and laugh in the same breath because you know your feelings are part of the true you. You're the first one in the pool, the first one to speak up against something you don't think is right, and the first one to apologize. You're authentic, and you just want everyone to feel as at peace with themselves as you do.

## THE JOB FOR YOU

In our survey, the happiest Authentic Unicorns have jobs that use their interpersonal skills, give them the chance to live out their values, and require integrity and a high level of trust.

Consider these careers if you're Authentic:

- Artist
- Designer
- Chef
- Artisan
- Guide
- Welder
- Plumber
- Electrician
- Carpenter
- Clergy person
- Sommelier

As with all the groups, the same six workplace happiness factors apply to the Authentic.

### Having a good boss

As an Authentic person, you need a boss who is willing to push you and be as transparent as they can with you. You also need a boss who can support you when you're feeling lost (as all authentic people feel at some point) and remind you what you're capable of. They need to hold your hopes and reflect them back to you on dreary days.

"No one is perfect, and pretending to be is going to cause more harm than good," says youth minister Emily B. "There was one time when my boss approached me about something I had done wrong, and it wasn't fun. The conversation wasn't easy. But in the end, I grew from it, and it also allowed my boss to have more trust in me and my work."

## Work-life balance

There was a heartbreaking robot/sculpture on display at the Guggenheim years back. It leaked bloodred fluid that was essential to its function and was in a constant state of sweeping up the fluid in order to keep functioning. Like that robot, there's a certain percentage of Authentic people who can't help themselves. An Authentic person in motion tends to stay in motion, especially if you have high Purpose-Driven scores as well. You need structure enough to help you leave work at work, no matter how much you love the work. And you need reminders that being true to yourself doesn't mean sacrificing yourself for the job.

"I've put my heart and soul into jobs because I felt like I was the only one there. It was like, 'If not me, who?' and when that's not recognized and when help never comes, it's demoralizing. I left, but it took a while to feel excited about work again," says Steve D., a marketing manager.

## Making enough money

The Authentic aren't afraid to say that money matters to them. They wouldn't be authentic if they didn't. As an Authentic person, you need fair pay and decent benefits. If your job takes care of you, you will more than repay those efforts.

"More money is always nice, but feeling valued and being given the chance to succeed in my job is equally important, I'd say," says organizer Tonya G.

## Autonomy and flexibility

"Flexibility" isn't always easy for an Authentic person. You tend to appreciate the security of knowing what's going to be asked of you when. But autonomy is another story. The Authentic appreciate autonomy.

"I like that I can make my own hours, for the most part," says performance artist and workshop leader Garritt B.

## Professional growth

Authentic people appreciate the opportunity to learn new skills and progress in their career. Some factors need to be present, however, to make your professional growth enjoyable. One is making sure what you're asked to do is in alignment with your values. The other is making sure you have the mental capacity to do well. You don't like being put in situations where you can't show up as your best self.

Art therapist Amelia G. says she's felt this during stressful times at work: "I'm normally all for learning more and growing and adding skills to my LinkedIn profile, but there was a time when I was starting out that I kept getting more and more clients, and I felt like I couldn't serve them at all well and do the other courses my bosses wanted me to take."

*Meaningful work*

Anytime someone sees the light, joins the cause, or discovers something good about themselves, an Authentic person finds joy. Your work is meaningful when there are people who benefit from it or when you know your message has gotten through.

"It's a cliché," says school counselor Brenda O. "But breakthroughs are a real thing, and when they happen with one of my students, it's the best feeling in the world."

---

"I'm tired of this, Grandpa!"

---

## WHERE THE AUTHENTIC LOSE THEIR STEAM

Authentic people will give it their all and then some, but once they've crossed the burnout line, they've already set their sights for what's next. Your highs are high, and your lows are low. You've probably experienced this in the past: Heartbreak of any kind made it impossible to go back to something you once loved, even when that something desperately wanted you back. Be vigilant against things that steal your joy and sap your energy by forcing you to be someone you're not.

*Death by a thousand cuts*

Our unhappy Authentic Unicorns have fairly consistent grievances. Most express frustration with and lack of faith in management. They are overworked and feel like they've got the weight of the world on their shoulders. Some are simply in the wrong position.

Volunteer coordinator Jane B. says if she had more support, things would be different: "With budget cuts and new management, I'm consistently being asked to do more with less. I love my volunteers and know how great the organization could be, but I'm not given any tools to succeed."

"I just want to do my job as cheerfully as possible, but when your boss is the most doom and gloom person you've ever met, it's not easy," says Tyler S., a veterinary technician.

"It turns out I hate IT," says systems analyst Dan S. "Just because you're good at something in school doesn't mean it should be your career."

### THE HAPPY-AT-WORK CHECKLIST

Are you Authentic? Do you manage an Authentic person? Here are my favorite ways of making sure both they and the company are happy:

**Give them spaces to share their opinions.** Ideally, small spaces. The Authentic need to be heard, and if they don't have space for that, it will come out in any place they can fit it, which is not always ideal and can discourage other types and teammates. Make intentional space for them to share their thoughts but always with the expectation that their thoughts will be considered but not always decided on.

**Assume the best in the Authentic.** Sometimes their feedback can be harsh, but nearly every time, it comes from a very good place. Try not to take things they say personally.

**Give them time and support to figure out who they are and how they fit in.** They need to know how to step into their role uniquely as themselves, which may take a little time to figure out. Be patient as they figure that out, and help how you can along the way.

**Point out their strengths.** Encourage them when you see something that they uniquely bring to the table or when you see them living out who they are and having a positive effect on the work or the team.

**As you see the Authentic gain trust, which will most likely happen quickly, give them opportunities to lead.** This may not be direct people management, but let them lead something, like a project or a task force. They will be able to connect people around a goal quickly and deeply, and get the job done well.

**Ask them how they see themselves and what they think they can work on.** You may have observations, but they are also in tune with themselves and have a different lens that can be helpful in guiding and developing them and their work.

**Help them know when to keep working on something and when to stop, close the laptop, and go home.** The Authentic need to guard carefully against burnout, and often they need a little support in that. Make sure they know that you care about them and want them to be healthy inside and outside of work and not be running on empty.

**Make sure they know they can trust you.** And be as solution oriented as possible. They don't want to be dumped on with problems. They want to know that you are as committed, or more, to helping find and being a part of the solution as you are asking them to be.

## JOBS THAT DO NOT WORK FOR THE AUTHENTIC

You can keep that smile on only for so long when you're trying not to show your real feelings, so you're not going to be happy in a job where you can't be your authentic self most of the time.

- Sales
- Hotel manager
- Customer service
- Nurse
- Executive assistant
- Advertising careers
- Marketing careers
- Politics, unfortunately
- Influencer
- Reality TV star

## THINGS TO DO RIGHT NOW TO BE HAPPIER

If you're already in the workforce and you find yourself in a job that simply doesn't work for you or you're frustrated to be unemployed, don't despair. It will get better. In the meantime, here are some coping mechanisms that work for authentic people.

### Create something

The world can be a bleak, dark place, but you can add some light to your life by creating something. The Authentic live their truth, so harness your creativity into making something. Sketch, write, embroider tea towels for the family. Whatever it is, you'll feel good making something authentic for yourself or others.

### Lose yourself in low-stakes reality TV shows

During a particularly difficult time in her life, an Authentic friend of mine found solace in *The Great Pottery Throw Down*. "It's such a kind and gentle show," she told me. "You root for everyone, and you feel good about it. They're all just doing their best to create beautiful things. It's so earnest."

As a person who values beauty and intentions, you, too, will benefit from finding a low-stakes reality TV show. My advice is to look for the British ones. They have a way of creating interest without stressing you out, unlike the offerings we have here.

*Volunteer*

If you're not finding meaning in your current position, go change the world another way. Volunteering is the best way for an Authentic person to recharge and find balance.

There are plenty of animal shelters, community centers, and organizations that help the unhoused that would love to have a volunteer like you. Choose your commitment level and get ready to feel better.

*Meditate*

You're not used to turning your thoughts inward. You already know what you're about, after all. But meditation can make a big difference for you. Try a ten-minute meditation before going into work to get yourself in the right headspace, and then do a quick meditation when you get home to help you slough off the bad energy. You might not be able to change things at work, but at least you'll learn to protect your mind and heart.

*Get a mantra*

You may want to find a way to break the cycle of negative thoughts that swirl through your mind when things are bad. This is the perfect time for a mantra. Some of my favorites for the Authentic include:

- This is not my forever job.
- This situation isn't great, but it's only temporary.
- I'm doing the best I can with the resources I have.
- My worth is not defined by this job.
- Nothing stays the same; things will get better.
- God / the universe has better things in store for me.

Write it on your bathroom mirror so you see it first thing in the morning, make it your phone's wallpaper and lock screen, or engrave it on a pendant. Whatever it takes, you'll benefit from having an encouraging thought to repeat to yourself when things are tough.

## REMEMBER WHO YOU ARE

At this point you know yourself and the factors that will make you happy at work. You are a naturally happy person because you don't spend time and energy being something you're not. Don't lose sight of yourself, no matter how bad it gets. You'll find your place soon, and the hardship you're facing today will help you be an even better person in the future.

"Take the first step in faith," goes the famous quote. "You don't have to see the whole staircase; just take the first step."

Put your shoes on. You're going to take the first step.

## TAKEAWAYS

- You value creativity, communication, and connection. Find a job with opportunity for all three and you're well on your way.
- You're happy when others are happy, but be careful to avoid burnout. Make sure you have ways to maintain work-life balance.
- Your passion can be your career; you've got more options than you think.

# CHAPTER 6

# DEFTLY FINDING HAPPINESS AS AN AGILE PERSON

That is a canvas sheet—the most versatile object known to man. It can be used to make tents, backpacks, shoes, stretchers, sails, tarpaulins, and I suppose, in the most dire of circumstances, it can be a surface on which to make art.

—Ron Swanson, *Parks and Recreation*

We're meant to feel the seasons change. Can't you accept nature, Emily? Must you control everything?

—Luc, *Emily in Paris*

For the Agile, the next step isn't a matter of being an anticipator or prepared or even fast. For the Agile, the next step doesn't take any thought at all. It's automatic. Think of Helen Parr, aka Elastigirl from *The Incredibles*. She bends and stretches and changes form to not only be an amazing superhero but to protect her family. She's an acrobat, markswoman, motorcyclist, pilot, and so much more. Because it's just who she is.

Honestly, superpowers aside, think of most any wife and mother—or head of household—you know. They're among the most agile people out there. My wife manages seven children, two dogs, our home, and perhaps the most challenging of all: me. She plans flawless parties, has a killer backhand, leaves no detail unchecked, and is the heart of our family. And she does it without breaking a sweat, the picture of elegance and grace. You probably know someone similar.

But being Agile isn't solely the domain of the person running the family. Anyone can be Agile. Agility is diverse. You might be Agile dominant if:

- You're an Enneagram type 2 or 3 (15 percent for each).
- You're a high D in your DiSC assessment (as 32 percent of Agile people are).
- Your next strongest Vander Index traits are Solver (28 percent of the Agile report this as their next strongest) and Authentic (22 percent say this is their next strongest).
- Your weakest Vander Index trait is Connected (only 11 percent of the Agile are strong in this trait).
- Friends can count on you to be up for anything.
- History still fascinates you (31 percent of the Agile report this as their favorite subject).
- You have a strong sense of self.
- Obstacles never keep you down for long.
- You don't waste time taking things personally.
- You were a star athlete or the debate team's MVP.

## MICRO TRAITS OF THE AGILE

Our happiest Agile Unicorns share two micro traits:

- **Resilience.** This, to me, is the cornerstone of agility. You can't be agile if you're stuck on the last thing that didn't go your way. Or, as Taylor Swift put it, "Down bad crying at the gym."

  Regina W., an engineer, says, "I don't dwell on my mistakes. I learn from them, of course, but I take the lesson and leave the rest."

- **Growth mindset.** The Agile view roadblocks as opportunities to learn. They adapt easily, thanks to a growth mindset. They're open to new ideas and are more willing to take risks. This mindset encourages innovative thinking and problem-solving, which are essential to staying happy while navigating the unpredictable nature of modern life.

  Designer Alex T., says, "Having a growth mindset has allowed me to see every challenge as an opportunity to grow and improve. It keeps me motivated and ready to tackle whatever comes my way."

---

**THE HAPPIEST AGILE PERSON YOU KNOW:**

**SARAH FRAZER**

Sarah Frazer is good in a crisis. Any crisis. Close your eyes, pick a crisis. Chances are Sarah Frazer, our Agile representative, would be able to help.

Born in the North to Southern parents, Frazer has had to be agile all her life. She spent her summers in Memphis where she code-switched from "Mom" and "Dad" to "sir" and "ma'am." She deftly balanced the rigors of high school academics with the fun (but at times exhausting) responsibilities that come with being well-liked by the entire student body. Now a rising star in the Chicago pickleball community, Frazer is agile on the court as well. In short, she can succeed in any situation.

And she's proven that she can succeed in any field too.

**Double (at least!) threat**

"I get along with people, and I'll try anything once," says Frazer on what's kept her agile. These characteristics are probably why Frazer was selected to play a roller-skating rabbit in the school play, why she's been a bridesmaid in no fewer than twenty weddings, how she ended up spending the night in a remote Danish fishing village in the late 1990s, and why she was selected from the audience to participate in an orca encounter at a "really off-the-books" aquarium.

As a child, Frazer always answered "lawyer" to the question of what she wanted to be when she grew up. Her uncle Lannier was a lawyer, so it seemed like the thing to do. But when she got to college, she realized that she was really good at science. Not only that, she loved it.

"Medicine was never in my mind as a career path," she says. "But then I found it, and it was perfect for me."

Frazer became a nurse and climbed the ranks until she was charge nurse on the ICU floor of a prestigious Chicago-area hospital.

"I loved that we were dealing with real life-or-death situations. I loved knowing that my quick thinking and talent helped save people's lives. Nursing is a great job for someone who is literally and figuratively fast on their feet," says Frazer. "And I never stopped loving being a nurse. But I'm also an adrenaline junkie and ambitious."

After ten years in nursing, Frazer took stock of her situation. She wanted to advance in her career, and to do that, she'd need to go back to school for another degree. But as long as she was going back to school, she asked herself, was the hospital still the place for her?

"I knew I didn't want to be under a doctor for the rest of my life, and I knew I didn't want to be a nurse anesthetist," says Frazer. "Plus, hospital leadership is challenging. There's a lot of strong personalities with strong opinions."

A different path occurred to Frazer. "People threatened to sue us—both the hospital and us individually—all the time," she says. "So I thought, *Why not law school?*"

**Swapping ligatures for litigation**

Even as her overly protective dad had plenty of reasons for "why not law school," Frazer went for it.

Just as nursing offered variety and multiple directions to go in, being a lawyer gave Frazer options. "That's a theme with me," she says. "I go into careers where there's a lot of different things I can do with it."

Originally, Frazer wanted to go into policymaking. But the chance to use both her nursing knowledge and her new JD as a litigator for injured people was too good to pass up.

With hundreds of thousands of dollars in play with every case, Frazer's job was as high stress and high stakes as you'd imagine.

"It was always interesting. I was always doing something new and different. I loved not knowing what I was going to be faced with each day," Frazer says.

But after four years of being both fearless and feared in court, Frazer was ready for another change.

**Back to the hospital**

"It's complicated when your new job requires less time and attention, with only forty hours a week being asked of me," Frazer says with a laugh. "At my old job, it was high profile, super stressful, and I was on call 24/7. When you're stressed about not being stressed, you know you needed to go in a different direction."

So Frazer returned to the hospital, but this time as their lawyer.

"Before, I was representing injured people," she says. "Now I'm representing the hospital. I love it, and it gives me time to have a life."

At some point, says Frazer, she realized she needed to find something fulfilling for herself as a person. "Something that wasn't my job," she explains.

Frazer is finding fulfillment in her dog, Gertie; sourdough bread making ("I got into it during the pandemic," she says. "Just like everyone else."); travel ("I still have friends in Denmark."); and the aforementioned pickleball.

She doesn't know what's next and she's not bothered by it. "I'll keep trying new things and stop when they no longer are interesting to me," she says. "Honestly, that's pretty much the key. I never take a ton of time to overly research things. I just go for it. That impulse has never steered me wrong."

## WHAT HAPPINESS AT WORK LOOKS LIKE FOR AGILE PEOPLE

Remember Gabby, that papillon who blasted through the Westminster Dog Show's agility course like a guided missile that took the internet and morning shows by storm? That's what the Agile feel like when they're on top of their game.

For Agile people, happiness at work means being in environments that are dynamic, where their resilience and growth mindset can be deployed to advantage. They find immense satisfaction in roles that allow them to explore, experiment, and grow, both personally and professionally, ensuring that every day brings something new and exciting to conquer.

## THE JOB FOR YOU

Part of being Agile and happy is knowing your circumstances so you can know what your resources and limitations are. The Agile can handle just about anything, but they prefer to have some ground rules. The most successful Agile Unicorns surveyed describe jobs where this is the case, but where certain variables are constantly changing.

Consider these careers if you're Agile:

- Residential plumber/electrician
- Entrepreneur
- Security
- Copywriter
- Construction
- Architect
- Engineer

- Trapeze artist
- Bounty hunter
- Pilot
- Air traffic control
- Mechanic
- Seamstress/tailor
- Hospitality
- Concierge
- Cakemaker
- Event planner
- Consultant

Now, let's look at happiness at work through the Agile lens.

## Having a good boss

A good boss for an Agile person nurtures a supportive environment, fosters collaboration, and encourages creativity. If you're Agile, it will help you thrive by leveraging your adaptability and responsiveness to change. You'll feel valued and motivated, which leads to higher job satisfaction and productivity.

Tonya L., a copywriter, says, "Having a boss who has the same mindset as I do helps me understand and complete tasks successfully."

## Work-life balance

For an Agile person, maintaining a healthy work-life balance is crucial. As an Agile person, you thrive in environments where you can adapt quickly and respond to change efficiently. A good work-life balance prevents burnout and promotes sustained energy, which is essential for your dynamic role.

Gretchen J., an event planner, says, "It took a while to find it, but achieving a good work-life balance has made all the difference. I feel more energized and capable of handling the demands of my job."

## Making enough money

Making enough money is pivotal to maintaining the lifestyle of an Agile person. Financial stability enables them to invest in continuous learning, attend industry conferences, and acquire the latest tools and technologies that keep them ahead of the curve. Furthermore, it reduces stress and allows them to focus on innovating and delivering high-quality work without financial distractions.

Alex M., a software developer, shares, "Knowing that my financial needs are met gives me peace of mind and the freedom to experiment and grow in my role. It's a key factor in my overall happiness and productivity at work."

## Autonomy and flexibility

Autonomy and flexibility are paramount for an Agile person because they allow for the freedom to innovate and adapt to new challenges without being constrained by rigid rules. When you have the liberty to make decisions and customize your work approach, you are more likely to excel and deliver exceptional results, and be happy while doing it.

Shane S., a marketing strategist, says, "Having the autonomy to implement my own ideas and the flexibility to work on diverse projects is what makes my job fulfilling and exciting."

## Professional growth

Professional growth is vital for an Agile person because it fuels their desire to continually improve and stay ahead of the curve in a fast-paced environment. Continuous learning and skill development not only enhance your expertise but also keep you motivated and engaged in your work. By constantly seeking new challenges and expanding your knowledge base, you can innovate, adapt to changing circumstances, and remain resilient in the face of adversity, which is pretty much your jam.

"The opportunity for professional growth keeps me energized and driven," says Heidi L., a project manager. "It ensures that I'm always evolving and bringing fresh ideas to the table, which is crucial in my ever-changing field."

## Meaningful work

When the tasks and projects they engage in resonate with their values and passions, it ignites a deeper level of commitment and enthusiasm for an Agile person.

"Knowing that my work makes a difference and aligns with my personal goals keeps me motivated and happy," shares Chris T., a UX designer. "It's what gives me the energy to keep pushing boundaries and finding creative solutions."

---

"In another life, I would have really liked just doing laundry and taxes with you."

---

WORK HOW YOU ARE WIRED

## WHERE THE AGILE STRUGGLE

Autonomy, professional growth, and meaningful work are what we've found to be the most important for an Agile person's happiness at work. When these three factors aren't there, the Agile suffer.

### The freedom to choose

Lack of autonomy can stifle creativity and innovation, making the Agile person feel trapped and unfulfilled. Without the freedom to explore new ideas and experiment with different approaches, work becomes monotonous and uninspiring.

"I hate my job," says researcher Jordan O. "I go in, do what I'm told, which is never anything new, and try to make the time go as quickly as possible."

### The ceiling is the limit

"Get busy living or get busy dying" is a quote from *The Shawshank Redemption* that the Agile live by. So when they feel stuck in their jobs and their opportunities for professional growth are limited, they become unhappy fast.

"I'm so bored at my job," says analyst Kirya R. "It's going nowhere, so I feel like I'm going nowhere."

### Values not aligning

Finally, when the work they do does not align with their values and passions, the Agile can feel purposeless. Without this connection, their enthusiasm and commitment can wane, leading to dissatisfaction.

"There is such a disconnect between who I am in real life and who I am at work," says Gabe B., a machinist. "I couldn't possibly care less about 'the mission,' so it's hard to be excited about it."

## THE HAPPY-AT-WORK CHECKLIST

Are you Agile? Do you manage an Agile person? Here are my top tips for managing.

**Check in on them regularly.** With how natural it is for them to be resilient, the Agile are often holding in a lot of things in conjunction with getting their work done. Make sure they are doing okay in that and offer to help so their burden doesn't get too heavy.

**When new ideas come down the pipeline, invite the Agile into them early and often.** They thrive in test environments and being early adopters to something. They can also give vital feedback if you are piloting something before a full company rollout. If you do this, make sure to give them ample time. Sometimes people are given a pilot project as an extra above-and-beyond effort, which the Agile would be happy to help with. But if it becomes a regular above-and-beyond ask, they will be at risk of burnout.

**Establish guidelines and parameters wherever possible.** This gives an Agile person freedom to try new things within a certain framework. These people thrive with boundaries but not with micromanagement. Make sure you walk that line well and avoid micromanaging them.

**Give them a wide range of types of work.** The Agile love variety and can handle jumping between types of projects or tasks. Don't unintentionally put any limits on them. Often as managers we can do that to try to help them or support them, but for the Agile, they don't need protection from variety like other types might.

**It can also help to give them options.** Again, the variety doesn't scare them, so you can present many ideas and let the Agile be a part of deciding what to work on.

**Know what your Agile employee is most passionate about.** Do your best to give them innovative work within their areas of passion. Help them see connections to their values and passions as often as possible and encourage them in those aspects of their work often.

## JOBS THAT DON'T WORK FOR THE AGILE

You're Agile. Of course you need dynamic opportunities, autonomy, and chances to grow. Our Agile Unicorns report the following as being really bad fits:

- Manufacturing

- Coding
- Research assistant
- Librarian
- Landscaper
- Bank teller
- Horticulturist
- CAD operator
- Life model for community center art class

## THINGS TO DO RIGHT NOW TO BE HAPPIER

If you're Agile and you're already in the workforce and you find yourself in a job that simply doesn't work for you or you're frustrated to be unemployed, don't despair. It will get better.

Here's my advice for feeling better in the meantime.

### *Vagus nerve stimulation*

Agile people can get really frustrated when it seems like their agility can't get them out of adverse situations. If you feel like you're swapping "agile" for "agitated," try vagus nerve stimulation. Your vagus nerve is the longest nerve in your body, and it goes from your brain to your large intestine. It helps control involuntary and motor functions, but it also plays a big role in your mood. If you're stressed, your vagus nerve can get stuck in fight-or-flight mode. And that is not as helpful as your vagus nerve thinks it is.

There are a lot of ways for you to help your vagus switch back to the peaceful land of your parasympathetic nervous system, including:

- Yoga

- Singing
- Reflexology
- Cold plunge

Keep an eye on your vagus nerve function. It's a rising star in the health and well-being space, and your learning its secrets now will make you all the more Agile in the future.

## Consider it pure joy!

I had a friend a few years back who seemed to have a dark rain cloud hovering over him at all times. He couldn't catch a break. He lost his job, his girlfriend broke up with him—heck, I'm surprised his dog made it out alive. He was practically living an old country song. All the agility in the world couldn't dig him out of the hole he was in. But one day, he stumbled upon this Bible verse: "Consider it pure joy, my brothers and sisters, whenever you face trials of many kinds, because you know that the testing of your faith produces perseverance."

From then on, he decided to welcome each fresh disaster that befell him. It was almost a "Bring it on, world" type of attitude. Kind of a dark way to cope, but once he leaned into it, he was able to change his attitude and even find his circumstances funny. Things got better eventually, as they always do, and he came out with agility and perseverance to spare.

## Take the long view

I know, you're Agile. You zig when they zag. You're not here to step back and observe. But sometimes that's the only thing you can do. So things are bad *now*. Think about the last time you thought it was the worst. Can you even remember it? You know you've had crises before, but even if you can't remember them, you got through it. You'll get through this too.

## FLEXIBILITY IS THE KEY TO VICTORY

Be open to opportunities that come your way, and the best ones will surely find you. Your best qualities are what make you Agile—resilience and a growth mindset—and what makes you *you*. In the words of Elastigirl, "Your identity is your most valuable possession. Protect it."

## TAKEAWAYS

- Look for jobs that feed your agility, not ones that merely tolerate it.
- Avoid jobs that don't have opportunity for autonomy, growth, or meaningful work.
- You're flexible, which in some circumstances is a pretty major superpower.

# CHAPTER 7

# FIGURING OUT THE KEY TO HAPPINESS AS A SOLVER

If you don't like where you are, change it. You are not a
tree.

—Jim Rohn

How do you solve a problem like Maria? How do you catch
a cloud and pin it down?

—Mother Abbess

The nuns in *The Sound of Music* were, ultimately, Solvers. Maybe not at the beginning, where they were being so pointedly unchristian about their novitiate Maria, but they came around. Mother Abbess packed Maria off to the von Trapp household to buy some time while they worked out the "Maria problem," and lo, the solution was right there waiting, boatswain's pipe in hand. Then, as to not let their efforts go to waste, the nuns gamely allowed Maria and her new family to hide out in their cemetery while they committed some casual criminal vehicular damage to buy them time enough to get them to the Alps, climbing every mountain.

In the meantime Maria, having found a job that suited her better, set about solving all the household problems, from lack of play clothes to lack of singing abilities to lack of opportunities to showcase yodeling.

How do you solve a problem like Maria? Stand back and let the nuns, current and former, show you how.

Whether or not you're inclined to join the gang at Nonnberg Abbey, you might be Solver dominant if you:

- Are a possibility thinker.
- Say yes.
- Have been considered the "peacemaker" of the group.
- Are an Enneagram type 5 or 9 (each count for 20 percent of the Solver population).
- Are C (32 percent of Solvers) or S (30 percent of Solvers) dominant for DiSC.
- See problems as opportunities.
- Have Purpose-Driven (30 percent) or Authentic (24 percent) as your next strongest Vander Index traits.
- Have Fast as your weakest Vander Index trait (only 8 percent rank above average for Fast).
- Are the last to complain.
- Loved history (29 percent) and science (21 percent) best when you were in school.
- Will always try a YouTube tutorial first before calling a plumber.

- Successfully navigated your Model UN team to victory.

## MICRO TRAITS OF THE SOLVERS

Our happiest working Solver Unicorns shared three micro traits.

- **Imagination.** The Solver knows that they need to think bigger to find the best solutions. Consultant Maragaret T. tells us, "I haven't always been a solver. I am not a perfectionist by any means, and at times in the past, that has led to being okay with mediocre results. Too often, I would use the excuse, 'Good enough is good enough,' which is sometimes the best approach. But it often leaves room for improvement. My mindset toward this shifted when I started utilizing a powerful thought experiment. I'd ask myself, 'Imagine this project has turned out exactly as desired. What would we have done to overcome the obstacles and find a way forward?' I've found that asking some version of this question gets me focused on a positive outcome rather than the problems standing in the way. When I envision success, it's easier to work my way backward and strategize potential solutions."
- **Patience.** Sometimes you get a light bulb moment, and the solution comes to you instantly. More often, it takes patience. Alan C., a therapist, says, "I enjoy solving problems and taking care of things. The way I have improved or gotten better at being a solver over the years is to try not to react but instead respond with thoughtfulness and patience. Sometimes waiting is the best solution, although it's not always easy for a solver to give things time."

- **Discernment.** Often, the most important part of solving a problem is figuring out what the problem actually is—and if it's really a problem. Professional coach John N. tells us, "One of my gifts and passions is that of a peacemaker. If my own relationship with another person is broken, I will do everything within my ability to resolve it. I notice and seek the same thing with others who will invite me into their situations through coaching. In a recent situation where I was coaching a leadership team through an issue that was dividing them, I began by meeting individually with the entire circle of those who were involved in the issue, as well as the staff who were impacted by it."

### THE HAPPIEST SOLVER YOU KNOW:
### DR. SANDRA KHONG TAI

If you and your child have ever sat down at the orthodontist to discuss treatment options, your child has probably asked why they need braces at all when there are clear aligners that can straighten teeth.

Many orthodontists will tell you that aligners don't really work for complex cases or for children. Some will tell you that you need to get some of your child's teeth pulled. They might proceed with a plan that involves headgear, metal, or keys to crank. But—and this was news to me—it might not have to be like that. If you're lucky and if you look for one, you can get an orthodontist like Dr. Sandra Khong Tai, a solver who will find another way.

Khong Tai has always been able to figure things out. From making friends as a peripatetic army kid to writing the book on a better way to straighten teeth.

Now the world's preeminent practitioner of clear aligners and a pioneer in finding alternatives to traditional braces, Khong Tai says becoming an orthodontist was her plan from a very young age. "I accompanied my younger sister to an orthodontic consultation where the orthodontist showed us before and after models of teeth, and I was instantly convinced that that was what I wanted to do with my life: change smiles," she says.

Khong Tai is a citizen of the world, which always benefits Solvers, who are adept at drawing upon their imagination, empathy, and experience when finding novel solutions to problems.

Born in the UK while her father trained at the prestigious Sandhurst Military Academy, Khong Tai says, "I usually introduce myself as British by birth, Malaysian by upbringing, American by education, and Canadian by citizenship. I grew up a child in the army, moving around various army bases in Malaysia."

It would have been easy for a young Khong Tai to keep to herself and not try to make new friends everywhere her family moved. But instead, she used her experience to fit into different social situations.

"Coming from such a varied background has allowed me to connect with people of many different cultures," she says. "In addition to moving so often, my mother loved to travel, and she would bring us with her from a young age. So she instilled in me a love for adventure and travel." With confidence firmly in place, Khong Tai was always the star of the school plays and always up for elocution and debate contests. Communication skills and stage presence would pay dividends for her later in life.

**Strong mothers raise strong daughters**

Khong Tai says there was a lot of medical influence in her family growing up. "My mother has three brothers who are medical doctors, and my mother trained as a nurse. In my mother's generation, men trained to be doctors and women trained to be nurses." But Khong Tai's mother knew that her daughter didn't have to conform to those standards.

"My mother always said to me, 'You have the brains; don't settle. You can become a doctor.' I believe that a parent's belief and encouragement to a young child give them the confidence to believe in themselves and to succeed in life."

But, says Khong Tai, the journey there was not easy. There were plenty of obstacles and plenty of challenges to solve, even before she became an orthodontist who would ultimately solve so many problematic smiles.

"I applied as a foreign student from Malaysia to come to the United States," she says. The odds of getting into a graduate orthodontic program were extremely small for any student, much less one coming from out of the country. "But I'm a person of faith, and people of faith dare to dream and believe great things," she says.

Khong Tai was accepted to the University of Minnesota's orthodontic program, which was good news, but there was one small complication: "I was five months pregnant with my first child when I received the news," she says. "I ran to my mother crying, asking, 'What should I do? Do I give up the dream?' But tough mothers raise strong daughters. My mother said to me, 'I will help you. Life will be tough the next few years, but you are young; you will survive.' And I did!"

She continues, "When my own daughter graduated as an orthodontist twenty-six years later, also from the University of Minnesota, I said to her, 'Neither you nor I would be an orthodontist today if not for your grandmother.'"

Khong Tai said she knew she was in the right place as soon as she started graduate school. "I would sit in the lecture room or be in the clinic seeing patients with a sense of the surreal—yes, I am training to be an orthodontist."

### Seeing potential in invisible treatments

After completing her training in Minnesota, Khong Tai moved back to Vancouver, Canada, where her family lived.

"I had to take about five different annual examinations to get my license to practice dentistry in Canada," she says. "It took me four years to complete the process. Many times during those four years, I would question if I really wanted to keep going or give up the dream. But there is a sense of destiny and calling. God created us for a purpose. During those dark years, I don't think I could ever have dreamed up the life I am living today."

Khong Tai describes herself as an early adopter of technology, which put her on the path to her undreamed-of success. "I learned how to move teeth with aligners very early on," she says. "As clear aligner technology continued to evolve, I would attempt more complex cases with aligners, in some cases developing my own clinical protocols for treatment."

### Writing the book

While practicing in Vancouver, Khong Tai also taught graduate classes. The students she was teaching how to successfully use clear aligners asked for the recommended text to go along with the class.

"There was none," says Khong Tai. "So I decided to write a graduate-level textbook that could be used in orthodontic graduate training programs to teach clear aligners. My writing style is very clear and concise, and the protocols I developed were written in the textbook." The book became a phenomenon in the dental and orthodontic world and is translated into thirteen languages, used in teaching universities in North America, Brazil, Chile, Spain, Portugal, France, Italy, Turkey, Japan, and Korea.

And how exactly does one learn orthodontic techniques from a textbook? Look for the second edition of *Clear Aligner Technique*, which has QR codes to videos of the tooth movements. Problem solved.

"Today, doctors will line up for up to two hours to get the book signed and a photo op with me at dental conferences all over the world," she says. "Some of them bring a well-read, underlined, highlighted copy with written notes in the margins. I am deeply moved by how valued the book is. It's my legacy to the orthodontic profession."

After the textbook came out, universities from all over wanted to study Khong Tai's cases to find out how she managed to achieve such amazing outcomes with aligners. Since then, research papers have been published by the

University of Michigan, University of Minnesota, University of Washington, West Virginia University, and, of course, the two universities where Khong Tai is a clinical assistant professor: the University of the Pacific and University of British Columbia.

**Becoming a household name in aligner innovation**

Khong Tai is always happy to stand up in front of a crowd and share her knowledge.

"My first few speaking engagements, I went at my own expense," she says. "Eventually, Align Technology, the company that makes Invisalign, heard about it and recruited me to be an official speaker or key opinion leader for the company."

Then the company asked her to start testing new innovations before they came to market, which led to Khong Tai becoming the "face" that launches these new innovations. "I have helped them launch every new innovation since 2017, the latest one being the Invisalign Palatal Expander. This happened as I was already traveling around the world to give lectures at conferences and became an easily recognizable face in Asia, the EU, and North and South America."

Khong Tai says people often tell her how her passion for orthodontics, aligners, and people comes across onstage. She attributes this to how she values people, "even if they are little kids," being systematic and focused on the details, and setting a standard for excellence.

In spite of the industry fame and glamorous travel schedule, Khong Tai says the best part of her job remains changing lives. "The opportunity I have been given to travel all over the world, to inspire, lead, and mentor other dentists and orthodontists, who will then, in turn, transform the lives of their patients, is very rewarding. To see others catch the vision and the passion, you know you've made a difference."

But even more valuable is the fulfillment Khong Tai gets from helping her own patients. "It is giving confidence to a little kid to smile after correcting their buck teeth or underbite," she says. "We have seen kids that are quiet personalities, who don't talk much, who hide their teeth, transform into lively, bubbly personalities when their smile is transformed. Kids who lisp learn to speak properly after their bite is fixed, and it goes on. It's the power of transformation."

## WHAT HAPPINESS AT WORK LOOKS LIKE FOR SOLVERS

Our Solver Unicorns are, you guessed it, happiest when they have problems that they can solve. They do best when they are in leadership positions and have the authority and resources to develop and implement solutions.

Solvers are the collies of our Unicorn types. They see what needs to be done, be it herding up the flock to move them to greener pastures or alerting a biped to Timmy's well entrapment, and they figure out a way to do it.

If you're a Solver, you get frustrated by small-minded people. You can't tolerate "that's the way we've always done it" as a reason for doing anything. You need a job that will fulfill your need to sink your teeth into a problem and work it all out. Like a dog with a snuffle mat, the effort you make along the way is just as important as what's waiting at the end.

## THE JOB FOR YOU

In our survey, the happiest Solver Unicorns have jobs that require problem-solving, empathy, and keen analytical skills. Our solvers work with systems, people, and problems in the form of IT developers, diplomats, and consultants.

Consider these careers if you're a solver:

- IT developer
- Programmer/Coder
- Firefighter
- Marketing/PR
- Financial analysis
- Orthodontist
- Analyst
- Therapist
- Engineer
- Consultant
- Agent
- Coach, any kind of coach

- Diplomat
- Plastic surgeon
- Systems engineer
- Eldest daughter

So what does workplace happiness look like to you if you're a Solver? Let's look at the six factors.

## Having a good boss

Solver bosses are best when they help guide your solving style and optimize your talent. Developer Deia S. says, "When I moved up a level in our organization, I was quick to notice shortcomings in how the higher-ups thought things should go, and how that was communicated and carried out at other levels. My boss was open to all that I noticed, but with each problem, she challenged me to bring three possible solutions. This was ten years ago, and that boss has retired, but this continues to be my approach."

On the other hand, Mike E., a health care administrator, says having a bad boss led him to develop his solver skills better than having a good boss ever could: "After you have been on the receiving end of poor leadership, you quickly become aware of the issues, and you generate solutions to overcome those issues. Although it is painful, and certainly not something you desire indefinitely, learning from the mistakes or poor leadership of others isn't wasted. It can be harnessed for good. You learn to adapt and overcome."

## Work-life balance

You're always thinking, always curious and problem-solving. Your work life and personal life tends to intertwine, but when you're at your niece's birthday party and are struck with the solution to that problem you've been working on all week at work, it's all good. Same for when you're sitting in that quarterly planning meeting and the perfect batting order for your league softball team pops into your head. You don't need to be in a certain place at a certain time to find answers. Your brain is constantly at it.

That said, Solvers are usually able to figure out a work-life balance that works for them, and if their managers are smart, they agree to it.

"I was fortunate enough to have management listen to my ideas on how I could meet both my work and family responsibilities with a hybrid schedule," says literary agent Carrie J. "Of course, I made this arrangement before getting hired and included it in my employment agreement, so there's a bit of resentment on the part of my colleagues. To them I say, 'If you don't ask, you don't get.' Asking for the solution is just as important to being a Solver as the solution itself."

## Making enough money

Solvers need transparency when it comes to salary because if they can't see why a 10 percent increase in profit from last year doesn't translate to more compensation for them, they're going to take their talents elsewhere. Conversely, if Solvers know they can take action that will directly correlate with an increased salary, they'll find a way to do it.

James H., an engineer, knows that helping his company profit helps him profit: "I like to stay ahead of the game. I stay up on current trends and technology, and I look for ways to be productive and make money for my company because I know that will end up meaning more for me."

## Autonomy and flexibility

Autonomy and flexibility in their jobs is important, but Solvers also often thrive when they learn the value of working as a team, which is not always something they're immediately enthusiastic about.

George P., a financial analyst, says, "Most of my success in life has been due to my 'get stuff done' attitude. However, I have learned over the years that I can get things done in different ways, beyond just doing things myself. I have grown from an independent contributor to accomplishing goals through the talents, skills, and passions of other people. This has taken me on a journey to develop new skill sets related to delegating, trusting, and communicating expectations better. This approach wasn't easy, at first, but it has protected me from burnout while giving me the satisfaction of growing others around me in their careers."

## Professional growth

Happy Solvers know the path to where they want to be. They just need the freedom and support to get there. Plastic surgeon Jane K. says she's taken every opportunity provided to her to advance in her career: "There isn't a lecture I won't attend, a visiting specialist I won't ask to coffee, or a conference I'll sit out on. If it can help me advance, I'm there."

## Meaningful work

Solvers love meaningful work, whether the world knows of their accomplishments or not. "The satisfaction I get from putting together a deal where everyone is more or less happy is the best part of my job," says family law attorney Caitlin R.

"I find meaning in my work because I know it supports the greater good," says Karissa E., an infection preventionist. "It's an immensely rewarding job: I get to track down threats to public health and stop them from becoming a crisis. It's solving problems, it's learning new things, and it's helping people."

---

"Excuse me, Mr. Andrews,
but I've been doing the math in my
head, and it seems that with the
number of people there are on board,
there aren't enough lifeboats."

---

## WHAT STOPS THE SOLVERS

"Life is so unnerving for a servant who's not serving, he's not whole without a soul to wait upon," sings *Beauty and the Beast*'s Lumière. And while I'd argue that's probably not true for any kind of server beyond ones that are enchanted household objects, it resonates with the Solvers. They're not happy if there's nothing to solve. Or when the problem in question is ill defined.

### Problems with problems

Nothing frustrates a Solver more than a badly positioned problem. Whether it's because the problem is poorly or ambiguously stated or the problem is given more or less credibility than it deserves, Solvers can't do their thing unless they know what they're trying to solve for. Side note: How do you start to solve a problem? A friend jokingly suggested this mnemonic: MARIA.

Measure: Is the problem something you can measure?

Agree: Does the team agree this is a problem?

Right time: Is it the right time to address this problem?

Inquire: Do you have enough information about the problem?

Action: What action needs to be taken?

But Solvers can't always get their team on board with this kind of thinking, and sometimes the problem remains a nebulous mess. This is kryptonite for a Solver.

## Hero complexes

Speaking of kryptonite . . . Of course you can solve anything, you're a Solver! But not even Solvers have every solution every time. Watch out for thinking that you're the only one who can save the day. That's bad for you and your team.

"When we're accustomed to taking charge and finding solutions to challenges, we easily become critical of others and their ability to solve problems," writes Aimee Ball. "We start to believe that we're the only ones who can fix the issue effectively, while everyone else is incompetent."[1]

Things rarely get better from there. The solver alienates team members, and team members resent the solver. And usually nothing ends up getting solved.

**THE HAPPY-AT-WORK CHECKLIST**

Have a Solver on your hands? Here are some tips for managing them that will keep them and the rest of your team on the right track. If you're a Solver yourself, be sure to let your team know which of these tips work best for your working style.

**Invite Solvers into brainstorming spaces.** If you are trying to find a solution for a problem, let this person help. They will bring a natural and different lens to the conversation that will often lead to a better solution than what you could have had without them.

**Make sure they are very clear about the desired outcome.** If they know where we're going, Solvers can find easy, achievable ways to get there.

**Give them some time.** Solvers don't always have a solution right away, but given some think time, they'll come up with some options. Don't always put them on the spot; give a deadline for them to come back to you with ideas if and when possible.

**Give a Solver as much of the overall picture as possible.** They are taking everything they know into consideration, so make sure they have the needed information to make good recommendations. A fast way to frustrate a Solver is to give them a problem without all the necessary or known information. It's like giving someone a puzzle without all the pieces. They will be immediately demotivated if they come up with solutions that are off from center because they didn't have all the info.

**Know that sometimes there are problems or challenges on your team or in your business that it is not your or your team's job to fix.** This can be one of the hardest things for a Solver—to see solutions for a problem that is not theirs to fix. In these situations, make sure they have an outlet to share their ideas and that they know that while we can't always fix everything, we are committed to improving anything in our team/department/area of responsibility, and soon.

**Help them with change management.** A Solver will see the clear path to greener pastures, but the rest of the team or whoever else is affected by the change won't see it as easily. Help set them up for success in implementing solutions by helping set a detailed, intentional change management strategy.

**Encourage them to invite others into the process of a solution.** They can't and shouldn't own it by themselves, and they need to know that they need others in order to get the job done. Partner them with an Agile person on your team to create a plan around how to achieve the solution and work the change management strategy.

**Keep an eye on burnout.** A Solver will indicate burnout with how engaged they are when solutions are needed. If you notice the fire and energy dwindling in them, make sure to do a pulse check there and find out what's making them disengage and how you can help.

## JOBS THAT DO NOT WORK FOR SOLVERS

Solvers will do their best to make work any circumstance they find themselves in. But that doesn't mean they're going to be happy doing it. To tweak the aphorism, Solvers will *live* where they're planted, but they certainly won't *bloom*. Make sure you're in the best possible soil for growing happiness by avoiding jobs like these:

- DMV
- Animation tracer
- Bank teller
- Standardized test administrator
- Fulfillment specialist
- Quality assurance
- Mail sorting
- Over-the-road trucker
- Beefeater
- North Korean military personnel

## THINGS TO DO RIGHT NOW TO BE HAPPIER

If you're not happy at work, you've got options. And as a Solver, you have more options than most. You're going to find an out-of-the-box way to make life better for yourself. Keep that channel open, as Martha Graham would say, and in the meantime, try these techniques to make life a little easier.

### Hit the road

You know those memes of people solving any problem that comes their way by buying tickets to Paris? Of course you do; that's you! And you know it works. You might not be able to completely skip town, but even just an afternoon change of scene will help. Remember, you're always thinking, always solving problems. There's no "off" position on the solution part of your brain. But changing where you are, seeing new things, and experiencing new experiences can help that problem-solving mind of yours come up with new ideas.

### Get a mantra

"Not my circus, not my monkeys" is a good one. You need to remind yourself not to take on all the burdens you see. Some can be solved, some can't. Many aren't your problems to solve. This is going to feel like tough love to your Solver brain, but it will spare your mental health in the long run.

*Solve where it makes sense*

I've recommended sublimating your negative-about-work feelings for many of our types because it works. The world is full of problems. If you can't find satisfaction at work, there are plenty of other places where your abilities can shine. Look for opportunities at church, your kids' school, or even your own home. Didn't you always want different cabinets in the kitchen? Grab a sledgehammer and start solving.

## LET THE PROBLEMS COME

No one is better equipped to handle life's challenges than you. It might not be fun, and it might not be easy. But you were born with a gift. You've got the power of possibility thinking, so you're way ahead of the game. Even if it's a struggle at times, you've got this.

Take it from the ultimate Solver who faced challenges but also had his share of light bulb moments (literally):

> I have not failed.
> I've just found ten thousand ways that won't work.
>
> —Thomas Edison

(By the way, wouldn't Edison have been a great PR person? Way to reframe the situation, Tom!)

## TAKEAWAYS

· No one is better equipped than you to figure out your happiness. But that doesn't mean you're alone. Welcome collaboration every once in a while. It'll help you in ways you might not have thought of.

- Your Solver mind is always going. That's a good thing. Just be sure to know what's actually worth or deserving of being solved.
- Seek out careers that are predictably unpredictable. Monotony is your danger zone.

# CHAPTER 8

# ANTICIPATING GREAT THINGS

## HAPPINESS AS AN ANTICIPATOR

In the symphony of life,
anticipation plays the sweetest melody.

—Oprah Winfrey

Anticipation is the heartbeat of hope,
the soundtrack of excitement.

—Maya Angelou

In the movie *Mamma Mia! Here We Go Again*, there's a moment where Christine Baranski's Tanya murmurs in wonderment at the island resort their late friend Donna Sheridan built. "How did Donna know?" she asks, incredulous that anyone could envision having a tourist destination on one of the most beautiful places on the planet. "That that could be this?"

"I guess she just . . . saw the future," says Donna's daughter, Sophie, equally wowed at her mother's ability to conceive of a luxury hotel on the land she inherited for free along with a small fortune—land, we can note, that has an eerie ability to draw in a glamorous and glittering assortment of international gorgeous people. Including Cher.

So Donna Sheridan, as played by Meryl Streep, would be considered an Anticipator. But I know our Unicorn Anticipators are a bit more tuned in than making the mental leaps required to go from "here's land" to "Pierce Brosnan is an architect" to "let's make this a resort."

As I said in *Be the Unicorn*, Anticipators don't need to see light-years ahead, just a few steps. You might be an Anticipator if:

- You're an Enneagram type 1 (as 18 percent of Anticipators are) or 8 (which is the case for 15 percent of Anticipators).
- You're a high D (to the tune of 28 percent of Anticipators) in DiSC assessment.
- You've always been fashion forward.
- Your stock picks are usually right.
- Solver and Agile (found among 30 and 21 percent of the Anticipators) are your next strongest Vander Index traits.
- Fast is your weakest Vander Index trait (only 7 percent of Anticipators are fast)
- Every experience you have is an opportunity to learn.
- You excelled in (or at least liked) English class, as is the case for 26 percent of Anticipators.
- You solve problems by working backward from the desired end.

## MICRO TRAITS OF THE ANTICIPATORS

Anticipators share one strong micro trait that helps them see the future—whether five seconds or five years from now.

- **Thinking things through.** Our Unicorn Anticipators have some pretty big-deal jobs. (You'll learn about Randy Eckman, an astrophysicist, shortly.) The stakes are high for them. They need to anticipate before the "do" because the "do" is so extreme. It could mean whether or not millions of dollars in research and development pay off, or the difference between life and death. "My job has real-life consequences when I don't anticipate well enough," says Sarah V., an engineer. "So I run the scenarios again and again and again until we're almost positive of the outcome."

**THE HAPPIEST ANTICIPATOR YOU KNOW:**

**RANDY ECKMAN**

I wrote in the introduction to this book that success isn't about getting the "dream job" you had when you were little. Kids will tell you with absolute certainty what they want to be when they grow up, but very few of them end up becoming what their childhood selves envisioned. It hardly ever works like that.

But sometimes it does.

It reminds me of the setup at the beginning of *Indiana Jones and the Last Crusade* when our Dr. Jones is home in

Chicago, teaching a class, telling the students what archaeology is and isn't. "We do not follow maps to buried treasure, and X never, ever marks the spot," he says. Flash-forward some minutes and thousands of miles later to Indy finding the location of a secret tomb under a big Roman numeral ten tiled on the floor. X marked the spot.

For our Anticipator case study subject, it was a similarly straightforward quest for his dream job. He was a boy who wanted to work for NASA. He grew up to be a man who works for NASA. X had always marked the spot.

### The right book and the right teachers

For Randy Eckman, it was always about space. He grew up in Dayton, Ohio, the birthplace of aviation, so liking space made him a bit of an outlier. At three years old, he told his mother he wanted to work for NASA.

"I don't think she even knew I knew what NASA was," he says.

What made Eckman's toddler career ambitions even more impressive was that he didn't want to be an astronaut, which would have been the more obvious choice for a child.

"I wasn't interested in traveling to space. It was more about seeing what's there—learning about astronomy and telescopes and planetary probes," says Eckman.

In first grade, the stars began to align for Eckman. "My mom got me this book on astronomy for Christmas," he says. "It was a big picture book. And at the same time, we had reading hour in the afternoon. Everyone in our first-grade class would go off and read any book they wanted. And friends could come read with you."

Reading hour in Eckman's class turned into an hour of Eckman "teaching about half the class about space," he says.

The same teacher that helped Eckman become the resident astronomer told him about the Hubble Telescope one day, about how it had been broken and a team had to go fix it.

"I went to the library and got a book about the repair mission, and that was a turning point for me," says Eckman. "I learned how neat it was to be part of the team that helps build the stuff and fix the problems. That was the first time mission control came into my thoughts."

### Coming back to earth

Eckman says that working for NASA, specifically in mission control, was his plan until middle school. "We were a blue-collar family living in a blue-collar neighborhood. Not a lot of people made it out of town," he says. "My mom reminded me that the odds were against me. I probably wasn't going to get to NASA. My family was practical and wanted me to have a practical job."

From there, Eckman set his sights on careers that were still science based but "more down to earth, literally." *CSI* was a popular show at the time, so Eckman thought forensic science and working in a crime lab might be for him.

"I entertained that for a few years," he says. "But I wasn't really into the blood and guts and having to spend time with awful people in awful situations. It wasn't the science I wanted to do."

A documentary on the History channel got Eckman back on the path to space. "It was called *Failure Is Not an Option*, and it was about the flight controllers on the Apollo missions," he says. "I thought, *This is what I want to be doing. I'm good at anticipating outcomes, and NASA needs people like that.*"

## Figuring it out

The first problem Eckman needed to solve was how to get to NASA. He says the son of his fifth-grade teacher had just started law school, and he figured if anyone was going to know how to help him get on the right track, it was him. "I messaged him and asked what I needed to do if I wanted to work in mission control," says Eckman. "He told me to go to Purdue and study aerospace engineering. So that's what I did."

Eckman says he has no idea how that law student knew exactly what he should have done, but he did, and it worked. Purdue was the only school Eckman toured, and his tour guide happened to be an intern for NASA. He says he asked her "all the things," and she gave him her email address. They stayed in touch, and when his grandfather gave him a trip to Houston to visit NASA for his high school graduation, Eckman met up with the woman and got more advice on how to succeed in college when the goal was NASA.

**Beyond 4.0s**

Recruiters from NASA's co-op program came to Purdue, and Eckman wasn't on the top of the list the school gave them because he wasn't at the top of the class. Undaunted, he went up to them and gave them his résumé anyway. He was part of "a handful of people" the recruiters gave up their lunch break to talk to and was selected to be part of the program. At that point, he says, he hadn't taken any aerospace classes, nor had he had the opportunities others had in high school to learn advanced science.

"I didn't know how space worked, but I was glad they had me!" he says.

Eckman later learned that he was chosen partly because he was a music minor, which was different from everyone else. "They needed well-rounded people with broad experience and lots of different interests," he says. "Not just STEM backgrounds."

### Curiosity and creativity

After college, Eckman moved to Houston and started his first job with NASA, in trajectory operations and planning for the International Space Station, "keeping track of it, making sure they didn't hit anything."

Now Eckman works in mission design for the Artemis program, NASA's current moon exploration program. *Design* is the operative word because getting from point A to point B in space is not as straightforward as it once was.

"You have to be creative when the numbers don't work. There's an artistic component to it," says Eckman. He also notes that, even among his coworkers, Eckman is less willing to take things at face value. "I'm the one who can't sleep until I know why a particular solution works. Curiosity has caused me to go down many rabbit holes. I lean a lot more on the art than the science."

### Innovation happens when you like your job

When you're happy with your job, says Eckman, "you're going to be more productive, feel more encouraged to understand why. If I'm underpaid or have a bad work environment, I'm not going to take the time or try. Innovation happens

because people enjoy what they do, not from the despera-
tion of it all."

"It takes everyone to do space," says Eckman, "not just
aerospace engineers. You need people who do social media,
community outreach, business operations, finance people.
We need more people who are happy in their careers, whatever that career is. That's what's going to make the world
more successful."

When you hear Eckman speak so enthusiastically about
the job he loves, another movie quote comes to mind: "Don't
forget what happened to the man who suddenly got everything he always wanted. . . . He lived happily ever after."

## WHAT HAPPINESS AT WORK LOOKS LIKE FOR YOU IF YOU'RE AN ANTICIPATOR

Anticipators are cool, calm, and collected—at least on the surface—
and they thrive in jobs where the stress might be high and the pressure may be on. Whether that's as a bomb diffuser or the parent in
charge of the snacks at the big game, Anticipators relish the chance
to have their predictions come true and to be ready when they do.

An interesting feature of the Anticipators is that when they're
interviewing for a job, they're often thinking about their next move,
even beyond landing the opportunity in front of them. I recall my
friend Jim, who had what some might call the audacity to ask at
his interview, "How long will the successful candidate stay in this

role?" Jim got the job because he was thinking longer term for both himself and his prospective company. When you're an Anticipator, it just makes sense.

This is a tough one to assign a dog type to because, God love them, dogs don't exactly play chess while the rest of the world plays checkers. To me, Anticipators are the dogs that hear you get up off the couch and meet you at the fridge. Or the ones that stand by the door, leash in mouth, knowing it's time for a walk. And if you didn't know it was time for a walk, well, you do now.

## THE JOB FOR YOU

In our survey, we found that the happiest Anticipator Unicorns are ones with clear goals and unlimited freedom to find the best ways of achieving those goals. With, like I said, a dose of pressure and a soupçon of public admiration. Careers where we've seen Anticipators thrive:

- Architect
- Engineer
- Executive assistant
- Fashion buyer/designer
- Trauma surgeon
- Concierge
- Logistics specialist
- Pilot
- Event planner
- Production stage manager
- Project manager

Anticipators are always thinking at least one step ahead, so it's important that they see the six workplace happiness factors present in their work. If not, chances are they're already halfway out the door.

## Having a good boss

You can't play a player, and you can't anticipate an Anticipator. Anticipator bosses need to be as sharp as their employees and help them develop their skills.

Kendra W., a guest services manager, says she learned from her boss: "He taught me how to anticipate questions that would be asked in meetings or presentations. He was excellent at this, and I have modeled this through the years. You get better at this by knowing your audience and what type of questions they have asked and what they will ask. You also learn by getting stumped when you are not fully prepared. It is okay to say you don't know and you'll get back to them, but it's best and more satisfying when you have anticipated the questions and have the answers ready to go."

## Work-life balance

An Anticipator can easily fall into a rabbit hole of possible outcomes, so it's important that they're able to leave work at work. Says photographer Scott B., "Working to prevent problems is a balance between proactive prevention and avoiding getting sucked into a pit of what-ifs."

## Making enough money

Anticipators usually land on their feet, even if they have to take a temporary pay cut. Buyer Charlie F. says, "I left a company I'd been part of for seventeen years because I saw the writing on the wall, even though it meant less money and security. A few years later, it went bankrupt. I was able to anticipate the future, made a bold move to leave, and I am happier (and gainfully employed) for it."

## Autonomy and flexibility

Autonomy and flexibility aren't deal-breakers for Anticipators, because they tend not to put themselves in places where the dynamic doesn't work for them in the first place. They're also less concerned about flexibility in the workplace and more concerned about outcomes.

"Autonomy is important to me," says physician Holly Z. "Flexibility, not as much. I'm trusted to make the best decisions without a room full of other people second-guessing me, I'm happy."

## Professional growth

Anticipators are natural learners, so not only do they enjoy the opportunity to grow in their careers, they absolutely need it to be happy. "I can see the next steps for me to take in this industry," says Gemma O., an editor. "And if I'm not getting opportunities to get there, I'm going to go somewhere that will support my career growth."

## *Meaningful work*

When you're an Anticipator in one of the higher-stakes professions I've mentioned, it's easy to see that your work has meaning. But even when the stakes aren't life or death, Anticipators can see their work having positive outcomes. "The gratitude that someone has when you're able to produce just the right tool, idea, or solution is really fulfilling and reinforcing," says executive assistant Keith P.

## "YEAH, BUT YOUR SCIENTISTS WERE SO PREOCCUPIED WITH WHETHER OR NOT THEY COULD, THEY DIDN'T STOP TO THINK IF THEY SHOULD." WHERE ANTICIPATORS GET FRUSTRATED

Anticipators like to figure things out. They need a puzzle to solve, a case to crack. To them, any information they get is a clue to help them figure out the next step. While the rest of us are living in black-and-white Kansas, the Anticipators are experiencing Technicolor, taking it all in and processing each color on the other side of the rainbow.

## *Taking a back seat*

Anticipators are good drivers, both literally and figuratively. And as anyone who has ever been married to one knows, when you take that power away, the Anticipator loses their spark, and things go downhill fast.

"It's hard to watch adverse things happen that you know will happen," says Marc R., a logistics specialist. "You know it's coming, but you don't have the agency or power to change it. It was the worst thing about my job before I moved up in the ranks."

## *It's Debbie Downer*

Anticipators struggle when they're the only ones of their kind, whether it's in leadership roles or as worker bees. When that's the case, they're like the cow in that Gary Larson cartoon. She stands among her blankly smiling peers in front of a sign reading "J&J Stockyards," notable in that her head is bigger than the rest. The caption says, "Only Claire, with her oversized brain, wore an expression of concern." It's lonely and frightening for an Anticipator when they feel like they're the only ones who see what's coming. What's worse, people tend to not like those who raise issues. The Anticipator gets labeled "negative," and the whole team suffers.

General manager Kenny W. says it took a while for him to learn how to present information that didn't make him seem like a wet blanket: "I tend to be more detail focused and never felt the need to be the visionary in a workplace dynamic. I've been able to hone that anticipatory skill through working with leaders who are big-picture thinkers, who might not think of the caveats in decision-making. My biggest challenge, especially early in my career, was finding a way to communicate my caveats, warnings, and in a way that didn't throw cold water on my leader's goals."

**THE HAPPY-AT-WORK CHECKLIST**

If you're an Anticipator or you manage one, check out these tips for successful Anticipator management.

**Let them know if the goalposts have changed as soon as possible.** They are constantly thinking about what's happening now and where it's leading us to find the best way, and it is very frustrating for the Anticipator to find out that there has been a change in destination and that they didn't know about it for longer than necessary.

**Anticipators are fantastic at thinking long term.** They see the potential effects of something, whether that's an idea or a structure or a new initiative. Invite the Anticipators into spaces where you need to be aware of the challenges ahead and know how to prepare for them well. Are you expanding into a new industry? Changing directions on a project? Restructuring a team? Let the Anticipators help you see where those decisions would take you as you refine plans.

**Anticipators' brains run *constantly* with what-if or possible scenarios.** They want to know all the possibilities of what could happen, so that means they need to think through each one and the effects of them before they can turn off their brain. Check in on them often in their work-life balance, and make sure they aren't bringing anxiety home.

**Help them know what it looks like to "turn off" when you go home.** Give them an opportunity to talk things through and air their concerns so they can feel able to leave issues at work.

**Give them space to grow.** Anticipators are great at seeing the future—and this applies to their own futures as well. Make sure you're having regular growth and development conversations and are staying open and transparent in those. If you don't, they may forecast a ceiling for themselves and start making plans to leave.

**Anticipators are naturals at creating a logical narrative in the absence of information.** This can be good, but it can also be hard for them. Help them see that their perception is not always reality, and make sure you're talking through what is true versus what is perceived. Give them as much information as possible so they aren't filling in the gaps and creating narratives that aren't true.

**Help them to communicate their ideas well.** Otherwise they might be perceived negatively by those who hear them. Help them verbalize their ideas as part of a solution and not just why something isn't going to work. And help them see this too.

## JOBS THAT DO NOT WORK FOR ANTICIPATORS

With your love of leading and being right, there are quite a few jobs that Unicorn Anticipators have struggled with:

- Animal husbandry
- Farmer
- Early childhood education
- Accounting

- Assembly line work
- Therapist
- Prison guard
- Software engineering
- Billing clerk
- Phlebotomy technician
- Medical records technician

## THINGS TO DO RIGHT NOW TO BE HAPPIER

If you're already in the workforce and you find yourself in a job that simply doesn't work for you or you're frustrated to be unemployed, don't despair. It will get better. As an Anticipator, you've no doubt run all the scenarios you can think of, but even if you don't see a path now, you'll find it soon enough.

Here's my advice for bolstering your ability to deal with suboptimal circumstances in the meantime.

### Calm that overworked brain

Deep breathing exercises, meditation, and progressive muscle relaxation are all helpful to an Anticipator. Find guided meditations with plenty of imagery to keep your brain busy but focused.

### Move

As an Anticipator, you're especially suited to physical activity that's choreographed. Try yoga or even something more outlandish like an adult tap class or aerial workout. You'll get the satisfaction of successful anticipation with the feel-good boost exercise gives you.

*Get out of the house*

You might find yourself doomscrolling in your own mind, trying to figure out what could possibly be the right combination of moves to get you out of your current situation. And I'm not going to say it doesn't work. Sometimes it does. But if you're not coming up with anything new, it's time to go outside. "Nature," says Aunt Elizabeth in *The Great*. "All the questions and all the answers in a delightfully chaotic form."

Being outside in some kind of nature is good for you. In just five minutes it can regulate the sympathetic nervous system and reduce stress. It also helps boost creativity, memory, and your attention span.[1] This is especially helpful for Anticipators who might find it hard to switch off from a problem or worry.

## THE BEST IS YET TO COME

Remember, every obstacle you encounter as an Anticipator paves the way for eventual success and fulfillment. Keep your head high. Your ability to anticipate is a light on your path to a brighter future. As self-help pioneer James Allen wrote, "Work joyfully and peacefully, knowing that right thoughts and right efforts inevitably bring about right results."

## TAKEAWAYS

- You're smart, you're on top of things, and you know you can figure out any situation life throws your way.
- Look for opportunities where there's pressure, performance, and opportunity to shine.
- Be patient and know that you can expect great things.

# CHAPTER 9

# PREPARED FOR HAPPINESS AT WORK

Chance favors the prepared mind.

—Louis Pasteur

Being prepared isn't always—or ever, really—glamorous, but it's an unsung hero when it comes to happiness and success. Think of Hermione Granger in the Harry Potter series. She's at times a major pain, but the girl is prepared. And that's gotten her and her crew out of sticky situations time and time again.

Our Prepared Unicorns are ready to respond to unexpected opportunities and challenges with confidence and resilience. At work, this takes the form of being proactive rather than reactive and being able to turn obstacles into stepping stones toward success.

You might be a well-prepared person if:

- You're an Enneagram type 1 or 6 (24 and 18 percent, respectively, of the Prepared).
- You're a high C on your DiSC assessment (along with 27 percent of your fellow Prepared peers).
- You always need to check your bags when you go on trips because you just never know if you'll need six bathing suits and that going-out outfit that you've never worn once in your life.
- Friends don't worry about anything when they're with you because they know you've got it covered.
- You do your research.
- You were locked in and ready to go with multiple computers and phones when Eras Tour tickets went on sale.
- Your next strongest Vander Index traits are Productive (37 percent of Prepared people) and Purpose-Driven (28 percent).
- Your weakest Vander Index trait is Self-Aware (a meager 9 percent of the Prepared are also Self-Aware).
- Science was your favorite subject in school (26 percent of the Prepared say so).
- Teachers love you because you (or your children) always have their correct school supplies on the first day of school.

## MICRO TRAITS OF BEING PREPARED

We've found that the happiest and most successful Prepared Unicorns share three micro traits.

- **Proactive.** The Prepared are ready when the unexpected happens. Musical director Donna R. says, "I've always said that people won't see the work you put in to properly prepare, but they will see the results if you don't. Preparation is the best investment of time you can make, and you can't do it without being proactive."

- **Imagination.** You can't be prepared without the imagination to think about what could happen in the near or far future. And you can't use your preparation for good without creative thinking. Paul S., a manufacturing plant manager, says, "You must outline your objectives ahead of time—and you must know what you want to accomplish before meetings, workweeks, or tasks begin. This includes getting organized and thoroughly thinking through what is most important. That takes imagination."

- **Meticulous.** The Prepared know that past behavior is the best predictor of future behavior. They pay attention to details and use every experience they've had as learning moments so they can be even better prepared the next time. An early childhood education specialist, Paula S. says that obsession with details is essential in her work. "We do about one field trip a month. I have made it a practice to visit the destination on my own first and then put a plan of action into place for how I want the day to go. I meticulously go over every detail from A–Z. When the day arrives and something doesn't go as planned, because I have thought it out, we can go in a different direction, and no one is even aware that something went wrong. If, at the end of the day, my room volunteers and chaperones tell me that it all went off without a hitch, then I know I have done my part in being prepared."

## THE HAPPIEST PREPARED PERSON YOU KNOW:
### HEIDI PANNOCK

When you're a mother of four and a nurse, you get used to being prepared for anything. Heidi Pannock knows this better than most. The co-owner of a hydration therapy business in Breckenridge, Colorado, Pannock says she might not have always known where she was heading, but she was determined to enjoy the journey.

**Always nurturing**

Pannock describes herself as a born caretaker. The Southern California native says that becoming a nurse was always something she'd planned for. But even before she had the opportunity, she was using her nurturing skills for good.

"I was the family nurturer," she says. "If I wasn't taking care of my siblings or my own children, I'd be volunteering and helping others."

Pannock stayed at home with her four children until her youngest was in kindergarten. Then she registered for nursing school to finally make her career ambitions a reality. "However," she says, "life had its own plans. My husband lost his job, so I had to start making money."

She switched gears and became a surgical assistant. The program was shorter and allowed Pannock to start earning money faster so she could support her family. Eight years after that, a newly single Pannock finally graduated with her bachelor's in nursing.

Being prepared to handle when life took her in unexpected directions helped Pannock roll with challenges and develop a sense of what her priorities were. It's a skill she's been able to use to her advantage her whole career.

"At the end of the day, I want to help people feel better the best I can," she says. "And to do this as a nurse, being prepared is crucial." Pannock says she always has supplies with her and is always prepared to handle emergencies. It's the result of years of experience both as a nurse and having raised four children.

"I'm used to thinking ahead and planning for various scenarios. Whether it's at work or at home with my kids and grandkids, I try to be ready for anything," she says.

## Prepared for change

Pannock worked in labor and delivery in a hospital for most of her career before she started her business.

"I've always felt strongly about women's services and the health care landscape American women face," she says. "In many ways, women are severely undervalued in our health care system. So I knew I wanted to be somewhere where I could help and advocate for women, especially at their most vulnerable moments."

But, she says, it was difficult for her to stay happy at her job, no matter how many women she was able to help. "I saw firsthand where the system was broken," she says. "And I saw that I was becoming broken because of it."

Pannock began to look for ways to stay passionate and fulfilled without burning out. She became a travel nurse. Then, one day, after a particularly tough travel assignment, she called her best friend, Kathleen, who had been her clinical instructor in nursing school.

"I said, 'Let's start that infusion service we talked about.' Within four months, we were up and running," says Pannock.

**Prepared for the market**

Pannock and Kathleen had been thinking about starting an IV hydration business for years.

"For one thing, I love doing IVs, and Kathleen is really smart," Pannock says with a laugh. But a deeper truth is that Pannock was able to read the trends and prepare to fill a need that had never before existed.

"Research suggests that IV hydration and therapy on a regular basis is really good for a population that, let's face it, isn't really that healthy," she says. "Helping people on the wellness side of things enables me to treat patients before they need a hospital and reactionary measures. It's proactive and it's good for them."

It's also good for Pannock and her cofounder. "We're getting older too," she says. "This kind of work is much less taxing and honestly pays better than being a nurse in a hospital."

Pannock still works the labor and delivery floor once a week to help her "stay passionate about the things I'm passionate about." But she's more than pleased with the decision to start a business with her best friend.

"We didn't know anyone else who was doing this," she says, "but we'd been doing the research. We knew there was market demand for it, particularly in a place like Breckenridge, where people come for vacation and either want a wellness experience or want to feel better as fast as possible, before their vacation ends."

Pannock says that, aside from her grandchildren, her greatest joy in life comes from helping people in her work every day: "I love it when someone comes in feeling unwell and leaves feeling better. There's a unique charge to it, a give-and-take. It's incredibly rewarding to make a positive impact on someone's life. I'm here, I'm ready, and I'm prepared to help the best I can. It's the best feeling."

## WHAT HAPPINESS AT WORK LOOKS LIKE FOR YOU IF YOU'RE PREPARED

For someone who is Prepared, happiness at work is the culmination of foresight, planning, and a proactive approach to their responsibilities. Nothing makes the Prepared more satisfied than being ready for challenges and having effective solutions for them. They're happiest when their preparation reduces their stress and gives them a sense of control over a chaotic world. Our Prepared Unicorns excel in various roles that require meticulous organization and readiness. Their happiness comes from the confidence in their ability to handle tasks efficiently, the fulfillment of seeing their efforts result in positive outcomes, and the peace of mind knowing they are always a step ahead.

## THE JOB FOR YOU

If you're a prepared person, you're going to be happiest in environments that require foresight, detailed planning, and an organized approach. Consider these careers:

- Day care worker
- Nurse
- Teacher
- Wedding planner
- Tax accountant
- Patent attorney
- Judge
- Choir director / orchestra conductor
- Dentist

- Truck driver
- Home repair / handyman
- Skilled tradesperson
- Cosmetologist / makeup artist
- Reporter

As with all the groups, the same six workplace happiness factors apply to productive perfectionists.

## Having a good boss

People who thrive on being prepared appreciate bosses who appreciate planning and organization. They set clear goals, create detailed plans, and consistently review progress. By supporting a structured environment, they help their employees stay on top of their tasks and be ready for any eventuality. The happiest Prepared Unicorns at work have bosses who advocate for regular planning sessions and follow-up reports, ensuring that their team remains disciplined and well-organized.

Susan C., a teacher, says she had a boss early on in her career who helped her become better and more efficient in her work. "'Plan your work, work your plan' was what my boss in my first real career job told me forty-one years ago," she says. "He emphasized getting my weekly and monthly plans to him from the start. These were followed by reports on the application of the plan—i.e.: what worked and what did not. This discipline helped me become very organized and efficient in my work by reinforcing tendencies that were already there. I often reflect on him and others who mentored me along the way to help me become successful. For them, I am grateful."

## Work-life balance

Creating a work-life balance is essential for the Prepared. Setting specific working hours and sticking to them helps keep work from encroaching on personal time. The Prepared love calendars, planners, and task-management apps.

"I like to keep my boundaries crystal clear, for myself and for my coworkers," says Gordon W., a judge. "There are some circumstances under which I must be bothered at home, but I'm very strict about not letting nonessential things get in the way."

## Making enough money

For the Prepared, knowing where their next paycheck is coming from—and how much it's going to be—is a no-brainer. They need to know down to the cent what their income is because they need to be able to plan accordingly. And if their salaries aren't adequate, they're not going to stick around simply for the love of the job.

"I'm prepared, so that makes me a planner," says tax accountant Lamarr F. "I know exactly how much I'm getting paid and what other people in my position get paid across the industry. That way, I have solid justification for when I ask for a raise."

## Autonomy and flexibility

Autonomy and flexibility are crucial for the Prepared. They thrive in environments where they have the freedom to plan their tasks and manage their time without micromanagement. By having control over their work schedules and methods, they can optimize their productivity and maintain the high standards they set for themselves.

Kelly R., a project manager, shares her experience: "Having the ability to make decisions about my projects without constant oversight allows me to implement my plans effectively and adjust them as needed. This autonomy is key to my success and satisfaction at work."

## Professional growth

Professional growth is important to the Prepared. They seek out opportunities for learning and development. The Prepared person values mentorship, additional training, and any resources that can contribute to their professional development.

"Continuous learning is a part of my routine," says software engineer Trina S. "Whether it's attending workshops, earning certifications, or simply staying updated with the latest industry trends, I make sure that I am always advancing and growing. This not only makes me a better professional but also enriches my work life."

## Meaningful work

For the Prepared, meaningful work is paramount. They need to feel that their efforts contribute to a greater purpose and that their role has a significant impact. The sense of fulfillment derived from meaningful work drives their motivation and commitment.

"I need to know that what I do makes a difference," explains health care consultant Jamie L. "Whether it's improving patient outcomes or streamlining health care processes, the value of my work is what keeps me engaged and passionate about my career."

---

"Grusha, you're a good soul. But you
know you're not too bright. I tell you if he
had the plague it couldn't be worse."[1]

---

## WHERE THE
## PREPARED STRUGGLE

Prepared people struggle when they feel like they're playing chess when the rest of the team is playing checkers. They can only do so much to compensate for what they sometimes perceive as team members' lack of organization and readiness.

*Bogged down in bureaucracy*
*and pulling more than their weight*

Dealing with bureaucracy and freeloaders at work can be incredibly frustrating for anyone, but particularly the Prepared.

"You find yourself constantly bogged down in endless paperwork, unnecessary meetings, and red tape that seems to serve no purpose but to hinder productivity. Meanwhile, you notice some of your colleagues shirking their responsibilities, leaving you to pick up the slack. I can't stand it," says VA caseworker Bryan G.

"I've since moved on," says former government employee Brad V. "But I used to get so frustrated when there was a decision to be made and we had to have fifteen meetings to make it happen. To cope, I began preparing packets to address the most likely options, and then the information was readily available when we were in the meeting. It took several times of being extremely frustrated before reaching that point. I determined that I could either complain about how it happened every time or I could find a solution. Ultimately, the solution turned out to be leaving that job."

## THE HAPPY-AT-WORK CHECKLIST

If you or someone you know is a Prepared person, check this list of best practices for Prepared management.

**Give a heads-up any opportunity you can.** The Prepared Unicorn doesn't enjoy having to process all aspects of a decision or new initiative and so on in real time. If possible, let them know if something new is coming so they can more easily make the shift in themselves to be accepting of the change.

**Help them in moments where you don't have advanced warning.** It's just part of life to be caught off guard when change happens. Sometimes a new idea comes, and you have to shift priorities immediately, or a staff change happens that is not public knowledge. In those moments where they feel caught off guard, make sure to create space for them to process the change with you if they want, and help them create a plan to feel like they are back on track and prepared to head in a new direction.

**When something inevitably changes, make sure the why is very clear.** Also, make sure it's known how much intentionality went into the decision. Sometimes Prepared people have a hard time trusting other people's preparedness if they weren't involved in the planning, so doing everything to show your and your organization's work can go a long way.

**Invite them to be a part of anything planning related.** Event planning, change management plans, intentional messaging, scheduling meetings or retreats—the Prepared can help with these. Prepared people thrive in spaces where their skill of seeing all the potential obstacles or grenades can be used to make the best plan, and they love seeing people move through the plans they prepared with ease and success.

**Any scenario where you are trying to make order out of chaos.** Invite the Prepared person into that. Not only will they be able to help with the solution, but they will also devise a very careful plan on how to get from where you are to where you're going that is most smooth for everyone involved.

**Give as much detail as possible.** Some types thrive on autonomy and freedom to create their own path. While that is somewhat true of Prepared people as well, they need to have as much information as possible to feel that same freedom to make a path or solution.

**If you notice your Prepared Unicorn stuck or stagnant, ask.** Find out what information they need or what obstacle they're trying to solve for, and help them get around it. Most often they stop when they can't see a logical way forward. This doesn't mean they're not doing the work—they are thinking through every scenario to get through the obstacle at hand.

**Do your best to anticipate their needs.** This may or may not come naturally to you, but as a manager of a Prepared Unicorn, you need to anticipate their needs to stay aligned with them. They are always thinking with a future lens, and doing your best to understand where they are and what might be helpful is crucial to keep them moving forward, whether that's more information or clarity or context to a problem.

**Have regular meetings with Prepared people.** They thrive when they know they have space to talk through what's on their plate and how they can be more prepared for it. Create a rhythm that makes sense for your work and stick to that for all your meetings.

## JOBS THAT DO NOT WORK
## FOR THE PREPARED

Roles that often involve high levels of spontaneity and require a more flexible approach can be challenging for those who thrive on meticulous planning and organization. Careers that might not work well for the Prepared include:

- Entrepreneur
- Commission-only sales jobs
- Freelance creative
- Customer service
- Journalism
- Athlete
- Hostage negotiator
- Crisis PR
- Mental health counselor
- Web developer
- Graphic designer
- ER doctor

## THINGS TO DO RIGHT NOW TO BE HAPPIER

If you're already in the workforce and you find yourself in a job that simply doesn't work for you or you're frustrated to be unemployed, don't despair. It will get better.

Here are some suggestions for finding happiness for your Prepared self.

## Celebrate the small wins

Not everything is going to go your way, no matter how prepared you are. Recognize and celebrate the small victories you achieve. You don't have to wait for a big hero moment. Take the wins when you can. It'll help you shift your focus from what's not working to what is going well, at least for now.

## Make your own structure

If your current job lacks inherent structure and opportunities for your prepared ways to shine, make your own. Develop detailed schedules, set clear goals, and establish consistent routines to bring order to your work environment.

## Mind your mental health

It might not feel like the best use of your time in the moment, but the more you can exercise, go outside, or meditate, the better off you'll be. Give your brain a break.

## Do what you do best

You're prepared, so something that will help is investing in yourself. Work on professional development or get trained in something new. Being prepared means constantly expanding your knowledge and abilities, which can boost confidence and launch you to the next level in your career.

## READY FOR ANYTHING

As a prepared person, you'll be ready when the right opportunity comes along. Keep your eyes and ears open and take your chances when you get them.

## TAKEAWAYS

- Remember that you probably won't find a lot of coworkers who have it as together as you do. Be patient.
- You can't prepare for everything, but you can give it a really good shot.
- Seek careers in your organized, plan-loving wheelhouse.

# CHAPTER 10

# TUNING IN TO HAPPINESS WHEN YOU'RE SELF-AWARE

*It is better to conquer yourself
than to win a thousand battles.*

—the Buddha

As I type this, there's a play on Broadway whose protagonist is in every way the opposite of self-aware. *Oh, Mary!* debuted in the summer of 2024 with an unlikely premise: Mary Todd Lincoln, future widow of Abe, wants to be a cabaret star. And somehow, it works.

Among Mary's many hilarious, clueless lines is: "I'm so bored. Nothing ever happens around here."

Mary says this while the country is going on year four of the Civil War and her husband is struggling to preserve the nation. But none of that matters to Mary. She wants to be someone more than just the First Lady. She wants to be a star.

"How would it look for the First Lady of the United States to be flitting around a stage right now in the ruins of war?!" asks the character named "Mary's husband."

"Sensational!" says Mary, lunging downstage and flinging her arms wide.

Cole Escola, the writer and star of the play, explained in an interview, "She cares so deeply about what people think of her, but she has a huge blind spot and doesn't realize that people actually find her grating and annoying and hate her. And that is me."[1]

It's an interesting take: Escola declares Mary to be very un-self-aware, and says they're the same. But in saying so, Escola is actually being very Self-Aware. Kind of a mind-bender. And sometimes, that's exactly what being Self-Aware is.

You might be Self-Aware if:

- You're an Enneagram type 2, 4, or 6 (pretty evenly distributed at 12, 10, and 10 percent of the Self-Aware).
- You're a high S or C (36 and 27 percent of Self-Aware people are).
- You have a keen ability to empathize with others.
- You've been told you're an overthinker.
- You're an active lister who asks meaningful questions.
- You can often be found journaling or meditating.
- You have high emotional intelligence.
- Your next strongest Vander Index traits are Authentic (33 percent) and Solver (29 percent of the Self-Aware).

- Your weakest Vander Index trait is Agile (just 8 percent are proficient here).
- Math was your favorite subject in school (as reported by 22 percent of the Self-Aware).
- Presentation is everything to you.
- Performance is second nature.

## MICRO TRAITS OF THE SELF-AWARE

The happiest Self-Aware people share two key micro traits. They're observant and sensitive.

- **Observant.** Being observant allows the Self-Aware to pick up on subtle cues and details in their environment. This heightened awareness can help them understand the needs and emotions of those around them, making them more effective in their interactions.

  "I notice everything," says self-aware Jesse, a social worker. "My kids hate it, but I know deep down they're grateful. It helps me know how they're feeling without having to ask."

- **Sensitive.** It's one thing to notice all that's going on around you; it's another to be able to respond to it successfully. The Self-Aware are incredibly sensitive. They know whether to push or give space when someone is avoiding eye contact. They know by the way their boss sat down at their desk if they're in a good or bad mood.

  "As a member of an orchestra," says concert violinist Kim L., "I have to be able to pick up on everything that's going on around me during a performance; otherwise, it doesn't work."

**THE HAPPIEST SELF-AWARE PERSON YOU KNOW:**
**JENNIFER PAULSON**

At work, Jennifer Paulson, my company's COO, is known as "the people whisperer."

"People can be incredibly frustrating," says Paulson. "We have all the means of communication in the world, but so much remains unsaid. Everyone's bringing their own diverse experiences, analogs, and emotions to every situation, big or small. The key is to take this into account when you're communicating with them and respond accordingly."

That's how you gain their trust, and that's how you build a happy, highly functional team, Paulson explains. "It doesn't do any good to talk to someone in the way you would want them to speak to you. You have to do one better: Speak to them in the way that you know they want to be spoken to based on the knowledge that you have of them—whether that knowledge comes from a long-term deep relationship or just from context clues you've picked up on, such as their mannerisms or clothing choices."

**The perks of being the big sister**

There's not one right way to come into your own self-awareness. You can practice, you can learn from others, or you can develop it as something of a survival instinct from having been faced with serious challenges.

"I'm an oldest daughter," says Paulson. "So I am the poster girl for 'eldest daughter syndrome' that everyone talks about these days. It got me to where I am today, but on the other hand, it got me to where I am today," she says, laughing.

*Eldest daughter syndrome* is a phrase coined on social media that refers to the unique set of expectations and circumstances firstborn girls face in their family dynamic. The big sister is often expected to be mature, responsible, and in control of her emotions from a very young age.

"I internalized early on that it's better for everyone else if I'm perfect and do exactly what other people expect of me," says Paulson. "Of course I didn't know then that that's what was happening. Instead I just ensured that I was the version of myself that people around me wanted me to be so that everyone would like me. I thought if I was first chair flute, golf team MVP, class president, five foot six and 105 pounds, Miss Green Bay, valedictorian, and went to an Ivy league school, I would be accepted and loved."

But the path to self-awareness isn't always linked to being an overachiever. For Paulson, gaining self-awareness came about by mastering the skill of guessing what everyone was thinking at all times.

"That way," she says, "I could act how they wanted me to. It's an incredibly transferable skill, really."

**Crashing, burning, and discovering her gifts**

As so often happens with gifted children, Paulson graduated from college, finished grad school, and then had no idea what to do.

"I knew what other people wanted me to do, but I had no idea what I actually wanted," she says. "I was so self-aware, so concerned about external expectations of me, that there really wasn't a 'self' there anymore."

Paulson packed up her University of Chicago graduate dorm room and moved in with her sister in New York City. With no money and no plan, she looked for a job.

"I've always loved potions and nice smelling things and beauty products," she says. "So when a Lush store on the Upper West Side had a help-wanted sign out, I went for it."

Paulson started as the most overqualified manager-in-training in the history of the company. While she was assembling and managing her team, she began to realize that she was good at her job because of something more than education.

"No matter where these kids—they were mostly teenagers and college students—came from, I was always able to tell what they were thinking and feeling. And I'd communicate in a way that made them feel safe and heard," she says. "It was about presenting myself in a way that was authentic to me but also made people feel comfortable. It's what Dale

Carnegie taught: Make the other person feel important—and do it sincerely."

### Rocketing up the corporate ladder

In two weeks, Paulson was named store manager. In nine months, she was promoted to manager of Lush's highest volume store. And four years later she was in corporate; in charge of the retail profit of all 250 of Lush's retail stores.

Paulson estimates that she's directly managed more than four hundred people in her career, including our team in her current position as COO of Vanderbloemen.

"I love mentoring people," she says. "I always tell my sister, 'If you do exactly what I say, you'll be happy, healthy, and thriving.' I can't say that to my employees, but I hope they pick up on a little of that!"

### Reading people

"I will tell you this today, and I'll tell you this ten years from now. If you'd asked me ten years ago, I'd say the same thing," says Paulson. "The most important skill you can have in life—work, life, whatever—is emotional intelligence. And you can't have that unless you have a healthy amount of self-awareness."

Self-awareness, says Paulson, is what drives life forward. "If you can be aware of how you're making another person feel," she says, "you're going to close more deals, build more meaningful relationships, and accomplish so much more than you would if you bulldoze into a situation."

Paulson says she's been able to de-escalate tense situations, help broker peace between warring department heads, and make sure everyone's voice was heard, even when they weren't speaking up.

"I remember a time when I was doing a six-month contract consulting for a manufacturing company," she says. "The leadership there was an absolute mess. We were in a meeting, and one of the 'bigger personalities' was insisting on a way forward and also insisting that everyone was on board with it. It was obvious to me that what he was saying wasn't true. The plan was bad, and no one was on board."

Paulson spoke up and said that at least one colleague, Brittany, was not in agreement. "I knew her well enough to know that she would appreciate me speaking up. So I said, 'Brittany is worried about this plan, and I can tell you exactly what she's thinking.' So I did, and it was, to a word, exactly what she was thinking."

"It's about knowing yourself so that you can know others," she says. "That's what being self-aware means to me."

### Finding a balance

While self-awareness is good, there is a point at which too much self-awareness becomes debilitating.

"It can be something like in a sci-fi movie where the mind reader is just flooded with information," says Paulson. "I'm wearing this, I'm in this place, I'm with these people, we're doing this activity, person A is thinking this, person B is thinking this, person C is just hungry and about to get hangry. Stuff like that. I had to learn to be a little less aware to avoid becoming neurotic. It's a balance for sure."

Paulson recalls, "My family makes fun of me sometimes for caring too much about how I think I'm making others feel. And sometimes I need to be asked multiple times to do something that I worry will make me look like a show-off. It's like, 'Do they really want me to play the piano at the party or are they just being nice?'"

Experience has taught Paulson to trust more and worry less.

"I'll always be able to tell how I'm coming across in a conversation," she says. "I'll always be able to have a pretty good idea of what the other person is feeling. But the more I experience life, the more I realize that it doesn't always matter. Sometimes the most important person to please is yourself."

## WHAT HAPPINESS AT WORK LOOKS LIKE FOR THE SELF-AWARE

The happiest Self-Aware Unicorns thrive in jobs where they know their self-awareness is guiding them in the right direction.

"When I can see that I've read the situation correctly," says life coach Danielle K., "it's really empowering. It feeds into my desire to help more and really key in on a project."

At the same time, the Self-Aware can be almost too aware, so it's best when they're in steady environments that aren't liable to change too much. Offices, remote work, the location doesn't matter as much as, as my kids would say, "the vibes." The day-to-day tasks can change, as long as the people and environment stay stable.

## THE JOB FOR YOU

Part of being self-aware, a big part of it—in fact, it's almost the definition—-is knowing your limitations. The Self-Aware can be successful in any position. They're chameleons that way, but some positions will make them happier than others.

Consider these top careers for the Self-Aware:

- Life coach
- Yoga instructor
- Social worker
- Actor
- Model
- Human resources
- Sales
- Mediator

- Classical musician
- Consultant
- Project manager
- Hostage negotiator

Here's how the six factors that make up workplace happiness work for the Self-Aware.

## Having a good boss

For a Self-Aware person, having a good boss means working under someone who respects their individuality and provides constructive feedback. A good boss creates an environment where their Self-Aware employee feels understood, which is crucial for them, since the Self-Aware employee will certainly know if things are "off."

"I think I speak for a lot of Self-Aware people when I say that we want feedback and can take constructive criticism because we don't take things too personally," says sales manager Keith P.

## Work-life balance

Work-life balance is important for the Self-Aware because, let's face it, being Self-Aware can be exhausting.

"I love my team, but if I have a full day of work and it's particularly busy and then there's a happy hour after work, I'm bailing," says marketing executive Isabel T. "I don't have that much charge left in my social battery."

## Making enough money

Making enough money helps the Self-Aware know they're on the right track. What's more, they know their worth and that they've got something special in their above average self-awareness.

"Sometimes I feel like a mind reader," says Brett Q., a broker, "which makes me really good at my job, which also makes me really valuable to my company."

## Autonomy and flexibility

Having the freedom to respond to a situation as they see fit is essential to a Self-Aware person. Because, more than likely, their way will be more nuanced and effective than anything you might have thought of.

"I have a lot of freedom and flexibility," says Max S., a counselor. "It shows that I'm trusted, which makes me more invested in the job."

## Professional growth

The Self-Aware know that there's always room for improvement, whether it's in themselves or in their career. They appreciate professional growth opportunities because it gives them greater insight into the world around them.

"Knowing that I'll have the chance to learn the next new way to manage people or be trained on a shiny new piece of technology is really exciting to me," says sales coordinator Reese B.

*Meaningful work*

Self-Aware people find meaning and purpose in their work when they see the positive results from their ability to read people.

"When you know how to connect with others and how to make them feel at ease, with psychological safety, then you get to the breakthroughs," says Henrik J., a school psychologist.

---

"She's my friend because we both
know what it's like to have people
be jealous of us."

---

## WHERE THE SELF-AWARE STRUGGLE

The Self-Aware rely on their ability to read people to succeed at their job. When they don't have the opportunity to do this, it doesn't always work out.

*When they're flying blind*

The Self-Aware don't need to be in the office to be successful, but they do need face time with their coworkers.

"If it's not an in-person meeting, I'll always ask that it be a video meeting, not just a phone call," says Helen W., a marketing specialist. "That way I can take visual cues from their facial expressions and reactions. If I'm on the phone, I feel like I'm flying blind. I need to be able to read the other person to make sure all our goals are accomplished."

"I had to do customer service in college," says sales associate Jim H. "I was terrible at it. I think if it had been in person, I'd have done better. But it was phone calls and chat functions. No one benefited from me doing that."

## When there's cognitive dissonance

The Self-Aware know what you're thinking. So when you say and do something different, it's not easy to compute.

"My boss says one thing and does another," says HR rep Annika T. "I can't stand it, because it's usually morally questionable and because, for some reason, it always takes me by surprise."

At the same time, the Self-Aware know what they're about. So when they're in a job that asks them to do something that goes against their values, they can struggle to the point of crisis.

"When I worked as a server, there was a time when management wanted to overhaul our uniforms to copycat a certain famous wings place," says Shannon, COO for an auction house. "I was in knots about it because I wanted to be a good employee, but no way was I comfortable wearing what they were suggesting. Luckily, enough of us pushed back that it didn't end up happening."

## When they get burned out

With so many points of information coming at them at all times, the Self-Aware can fatigue fast. If that happens, they lose their ability to be observant and sensitive. They start missing the forest for the trees.

"Early on, I had a job as an intake nurse at a really busy emergency department," says Noah R., now a hospital administrator. "I thought it was perfect for me because I'm really empathetic, and I don't miss a thing. Turns out, it was a nightmare for me because I'm really empathetic and don't miss a thing. It was just too overwhelming. I'd come home and have to sit in silence for like half an hour before I could deal with talking to people again."

## THE HAPPY-AT-WORK CHECKLIST

If being self-aware is your superpower or you work with those who are Self-Aware, consider these management hacks to make sure everyone is content:

**Create an environment of stability and safety for the Self-Aware.** They are constantly reading their environment, knowing how best to show up for people and for certain situations, and they need to have a space to guarantee they can show up as just them and be accepted—to not have to carry the weight of how they're perceived.

**Have them give you a regular pulse check on how they're doing and how they want to grow and improve.** They are going to have more action items for themselves than you would be able to come up with for them, so work together on the things they want to improve on themselves. And weave your feedback into these conversations.

**Make sure these meetings and others are face-to-face if possible.** This type thrives on people interaction, and removing their senses and ability to "read the room" can make things significantly more difficult for them.

**Self-Aware people are their own worst critics, so encourage them often.** Words of affirmation mean a lot to the Self-Aware, so any opportunities to give genuine feedback—big or small, in writing or spoken—will mean a great deal to them.

**If the Self-Aware is someone you can trust, ask them for feedback on your leadership.** If someone is going to know your strengths and weaknesses and see how they fit into the overall team, organization, or whatever, it's the Self-Aware.

**If you are trying to figure out a communication plan or messaging for something or the right way to deliver information, invite the Self-Aware into these projects.** They will know how the recipient of the information will receive it, which is vital to a successful communication plan.

**Always be honest with this type.** The Self-Aware can read honesty and authenticity on anyone and will struggle if what they perceive and what they're told don't match. Make sure you are honest with them, and if you're in a situation where you see they have this gap between perception and actions, give them space with you to process that.

**Make sure they have space to recharge.** They are good at reading people and situations, but that also means they hold a lot of emotional weight for everyone around them.

Make sure that they're not taking on too much and that they have space and time to remove themselves from those situations and recharge.

## JOBS THAT DO NOT WORK FOR THE SELF-AWARE

The Self-Aware, as I've said, are like chameleons. They can fit in anywhere, but it takes a certain number of boxes checked for them to be happy. The least happy Self-Aware surveyed worked in these types of jobs:

- Government
- Telemarketing
- Park ranger
- Computer programmer
- Game designer
- Judge
- Receptionist

## THINGS TO DO RIGHT NOW TO BE HAPPIER

Life can be pretty uncomfortable for a Self-Aware person who is also unhappy. If you have a job that's not bringing you joy or you're getting annoyed that you still haven't found any job at all, try to be patient. What's meant for you will find you.

And in the meantime, try these tactics.

## *Eliminate what doesn't work*

Even if you can't change your job or employment circumstances, you can take steps to feel more aligned with yourself. Start with what you can change. Consider doing a thorough sort, and eliminate anything from these categories that doesn't make you feel like your best self:

- Clothes
- Shoes
- Decor
- Makeup/grooming products

Then think more in the abstract. Are there any commitments or obligations you have that just don't fit with your sense of self? How soon can you step away from that board or wrap up your volunteer work? Are there relationships that haven't served you in years? It might be time to purge those too.

## *Self-Care for the Self-Aware*

Be sure to take care of yourself during these stressful times, starting with making sure you're validating yourself and your feelings. Then get out in nature, buy a new moisturizer (you might need to replace yours anyway), and generally indulge in any li'l treats you deem necessary for the time being. You've got to keep up your spirits so when the prefect opportunity comes along you'll be ready!

## THE ANSWER IS YOU

You've always been able to use your gifts as a Self-Aware person for the benefit of others. Now it's time to start using them for your own benefit too. You might not be able to have "it all," but you can certainly have that. In the real words of Mary's husband, Abraham Lincoln, "You have confidence in yourself, which is a valuable, if not an indispensable, quality."

## TAKEAWAYS

- Being self-aware means being able to tell what's going on in other minds too.
- Avoid jobs where you can't interface with people.
- Remember that what makes you so amazing can also drain you; take care to avoid burnout.

# CHAPTER 11

# THE CURIOUS AND CURIOUSER AT WORK

Of the gladdest moments in human life, methinks, is the departure upon a distant journey into unknown lands.

—Sir Richard Francis Burton

But she came from Greece. She had a thirst for knowledge. It couldn't have been me. I've never wanted to know anything.

—*Saltburn*'s Elspeth Catton, famously uncurious

Some people just know that everything's going to be okay. They don't know how, but they know it's all going to work out. And along the way, they're going to see everything, learn everything, and do everything they can. Because life's a buffet, and you won't see a Curious person going hungry. You might be one of them if:

- You're an Enneagram type 5 or 7 (Curious people are 17 percent 5 and 12 percent 7).
- You're a high i on the DiSC assessment scale (as reported by 38 percent of the Curious).
- You're great at parties because you're genuinely interested in learning about others.
- Your top Vander Index traits after curiosity are Likable and Solver (both with 22 percent of the Curious population).
- Your weakest Vander Index trait is Fast (only 5 percent of the Curious surveyed rank high for Fast).
- You like knowing the how and the why of things.
- You're a joiner and always happy to lead the office culture initiatives.
- You were a great student, but sometimes your teachers found you to be exhausting.
- Your favorite subject was science (23 percent of the Curious report this).
- The documentary category at the Oscars determines your watch list for the first half of the year.

## MICRO TRAITS OF THE CURIOUS

Studying our Curious Unicorns, we've identified micro traits that the happiest among them share.

- **They ask questions.** You can't be curious without fearlessly asking questions. "I ask lots of questions, questions other people usually don't think to ask," says Julianna A., a researcher. "However, learning how to ask *good* questions takes practice. Curiosity is a skill worth growing in, so my tip is to evaluate your ability to stay curious, ask good questions, and actively listen to others; be self-aware, and practice."

- **They love learning and are genuinely interested.** Dan H., an IT professional, says, "Every day on the job, I ask a lot of questions and am genuinely interested in hearing an answer. From these and other sources, I learn."
- **They pay close attention.** The unexamined life is not worth living, and the Curious make their lives plenty worth it. John J., an artist, says, "I find it natural to stay curious. I pay close attention to the people and world around me, assuming there is much I do not know but would be delighted to discover."

It's hard not to like a Curious person. For them, it's just blue sky and big ideas. Like a blue heeler or border collie, Curious people want to learn, solve problems, and need to explore. When they're in the right place, like running alongside their people or doing a job they love and are good at, their happiness radiates from them. But when the circumstances aren't right for them, they'll get sad, sullen, and surly. When you're curious and content, everyone will benefit.

> **THE HAPPIEST CURIOUS PERSON YOU KNOW:**
> **AMANDA HOWARD**
>
> Amanda Howard loves her job.
>
> "No two days are ever really the same," she says. "Curiosity drives you."

Howard works as an editor for a major US news outlet. The job—and her curiosity—have taken her all across the world. She's currently in Europe.

"Being curious is the absolute heart of it," she says. "Each topic is, in its way, a puzzle. And you get to explore and think of as many angles and questions you can ask, starting with asking yourself, *What do I not know about this? What do I think is true? What do I need to question?* And then you question everything."

## On a curious path

Good news for people who haven't always known what they wanted to be when they grew up. Howard said she stumbled onto her career path. Journalism wasn't a lifelong dream. She wasn't a kid reporter for her local station, nor was she editor of her school newspaper. She didn't even have a poster of Diane Sawyer in her room growing up.

"I liked to read, and I liked to write," she says. That was the only indication that Howard would be suited for a news-related career.

"But I was always curious," she says. "I grew up in America and have lived as an adult in both America and abroad. I've been curious about every place I've ever lived or have traveled to. It's been really interesting to learn new places."

Lots of people have lived in lots of places, but for the Curious, like Howard, the experiences unlock new chances to learn, more questions to ask, and better perspectives on people. All of this, she says, helps in her work. She says, "In addition to being really fun and interesting by itself, it's given me a better understanding of what other people are going through. It's fascinating to see, when you go around the world, how people are quite similar in some ways and in others really different."

Curiosity, she says, is the key to being surprised by the world. Our brains are wired to sort information and make generalizations; that's important. But, says Howard, because our brains do that, it's easy for us to make assumptions. "The more we can stay curious, the more we can allow ourselves to be surprised, and maybe pleasantly surprised."

**Always more to discover**

Part of what makes Howard good at her job—and why she loves it as much as she does—is rising to the challenge of being a Curious person relating information to other Curious people. Because, she says, people who consume news in any form are curious about what's going on.

Howard says, "You're trying to relay events to people in a way they can understand. You're always trying to give context. And, depending on the news outlet, you need to make it make sense to a wide variety of people."

"You're always asking what's not only interesting but what's important," she says. The pandemic was particularly interesting for Howard because of the many angles journalists took with it, most focused on determining and relating what was important. "We had not lived through something like it before. There was such a wide variety of approaches that were taken."

Whether it's health, the arts, sports, or politics, Howard is rarely bored by any topic, although she is partial to speaking with creative people and people trying to make the world a better place. "Getting them to tell you what they're making or thinking or working on—it's quite colorful. But no matter what the topic, there is always more to discover about what's going on," she says. "The more curiosity you can throw at a story or an idea, the more relevant it will be."

**About the people**

Curious people do well when they're working with other Curious people, and Howard is no exception. "You don't work in isolation. Your coworkers contribute their curiosity too," she says. They also add their experiences, backgrounds, and specialties. All of this, says Howard, helps create a more robust picture of the information they're trying to relay.

Howard says there's room for all kinds of people in journalism. "It's almost like the theater," she says. "You don't need to be the person onstage, just like you don't need to be the person out with a microphone in the aftermath of a tornado. You can find what's suitable to you."

For anyone thinking of going into journalism, Howard says to start out as she and most of her colleagues did: small.

"I started at a local newspaper, not really knowing if it's what I wanted to do with my life," she says. Staying curious, asking questions, and following where the answers to those questions paved the way to opportunities Howard never would have imagined.

"Journalism school doesn't hurt either," Howard advises. "They teach you the skills, which are changing because the types of output are changing, but the integrity of the process is the same: You're reading documents, you're listening, you're asking, you're being curious. And one advantage of school is that you get to practice, get things wrong, and figure out what you can do better."

"It's like anything else. If you want to learn how to cook, go hang out with people who can cook," she says. "If you want to be a reporter, hang out with reporters. If you have an idea, raise your hand and pitch it. The worst that can happen is you'll be told no."

**Staying curious**

Howard says she's happiest when she's helping people in their own curiosity. As someone who wasn't sure where her life would take her, she's curiosity's biggest fan.

"It's great to not know what you want to be until you get there," she says. "It's great to not know what your next step is. That's when interesting things happen. And if you're curious, you will find more interesting opportunities wherever you are."

## WHAT HAPPINESS AT WORK LOOKS LIKE IF YOU'RE CURIOUS

When you've got above-average curiosity, you thrive on the unknown, spontaneity, and that childlike sense of wonder people find either endearing or annoying. You need a job with questions to answer, opportunities to get your hands dirty, plenty of space to learn and explore new topics, and a team of like-minded people. Unlike other types of Unicorns, the Curious like you don't need clear objectives outlining every step. You need the goal and then the freedom to work it all out.

## THE JOB FOR YOU

In our survey, the happiest Curious people have jobs that require problem-solving, learning new things, a sense of adventure, and the ability to collaborate with others when they want to. Our Curious

Unicorns are journalists, researchers, and all kinds of professions that end in "-ist."

Consider these careers if you're one of the Curious:

- Journalist
- Scientist
- Researcher
- Archaeologist
- Museum curator
- Art historian
- Zoologist
- Explorer
- Marine biologist
- Geologist
- Software developer / IT person
- Astronaut
- Detective

So what does workplace happiness look like to you if you're curious? Let's look at the six factors.

### Having a good boss

Your boss doesn't need to be as Curious as you, but they do need to appreciate your questioning ways. Lab tech Jane K. says her boss saw and supported her curiosity early on: "As an intern, one of my supervisors recognized that I asked good questions. He got me a small notebook in recognition of this quality. It affirmed this character trait and spurred me to continue on the path of asking good questions."

Emile M. says that when he was in the Navy, he had to learn fast, and his curiosity was valued. "I realized that I had a lot to learn in order to be effective and to achieve the knowledge level and competence of most of my peers," he says. "I asked questions about everything all the time. My supervisor chuckled one day and labeled me as being 'in a constant state of professional curiosity.' While I thought he might be irritated by all my questions, he affirmed that this was actually a critical trait to success and ongoing professional growth. I often felt my curiosity was just an annoyance to others. And it probably was at times! But now I leverage it as a sort of superpower."

## Work-life balance

If you're a curious person, it can be hard to tell where your job ends and your life begins. But that's not a bad thing. And the Curious always find ways to make it work. Middle school teacher Lauren S. says, "It became very apparent to me very quickly that the kids I teach are not growing up like I did. Consequently, I have a lot of learning to do to serve them well! I love to read, but I have four small children, so sitting down and reading at home is out of the question. My friend introduced me to Audible, and this changed everything. I commute to work so I have time in the car to listen to books about teens, parenting, and Gen Z. It has shaped the way I teach, and I can't get enough!"

"I take work calls some evenings and schedule my kids' appointments during the day at the office. There's no work-life balance except to say that both get done well and it works," says event planner Michelle L.

## Making enough money

For the Curious, it's not all about the money, but making a competitive, living wage is certainly a plus.

"You can't do your best work when you're worried about money," says elementary school principal Claudia K. "I'm fortunate enough to work for a school system and community that recognizes this, but I'm sure I'm in the minority when it comes to fair compensation in my field."

## Autonomy and flexibility

Curious people generally like to be around people, but being in lockstep with any system or team is a hard no. You need the freedom to make your own schedule, if possible, and to work independently when you choose to.

"Sometimes being around my coworkers is exactly what I need," says Brian R., a systems analyst. "Other times, I'm grateful to have an office with a door that closes."

## Professional growth

Conferences, development days, and off-site trainings might be dreaded by other types, but Curious people know that professional growth is grist for their metaphorical mills. You have a unique ability to find something of merit in every experience or situation. You're pretty much always growing professionally, consciously or not, and it's even better when you have the opportunity to do so in Maui or Fort Lauderdale or somewhere else interesting. The Curious have no problem proving to their leadership that they're ready for what's next. They were born ready for what's next.

Coach Dave B. says curiosity has served his career development well, although loved ones might have to pay a bit of a price: "At the start of my career, I had a mentor who asked fantastic questions. I resolved to develop a heart of curiosity and grow the skill of asking great questions. From that point it was 90 percent practice, practice, practice and 10 percent pursuit of resources to get better at asking great questions (books, facilitator training, grad school work, and so on). When my teams experience success or failure, getting curious about why either occurred is standard operating procedure for me. I've learned that getting curious about subjects that are novel, new, or ones I have no experience with is highly helpful to developing and sustaining a curious outlook." He jokes, "I once talked with an engineer about LEDs for an hour. My wife still reminds me how painful it was to observe."

## *Meaningful work*

Curious people know that anything done with purpose has value and that all work can be meaningful work.

"My job is pretty behind the scenes, but it's satisfying knowing people might not see me, but they'll see my work," says museum curator Angela M.

Our data shows that Curious Unicorns are the most likely to change professions in the interest of learning new skills and trying different paths.

"I have worked as a paralegal, church administrator, office manager, executive assistant, financial administrator, real estate appraiser, kidney dialysis tech, food service worker, graphic/media/digital designer, and now I am studying to be a financial adviser," says Kristine B. "I am always looking to expand and improve my skill set. As my career opportunities shift, my curiosity is one trait that remains key."

---

"Never tell me the odds."

---

## HOW THE CURIOUS CAN LOSE THEIR SPARK

It's a running theme here—no matter what your personality type, when your workplace and colleagues don't share the same values you have, it's tough to be happy. In our survey, we found that most Curious people who hated their jobs were unhappy because of their bosses' and coworkers' ways of thinking, feeling underappreciated, and not connecting with the work.

## WHEN IT'S THE CULTURE THAT KILLS YOU

Nothing can get a Curious person down like an uninterested pessimist.

"We're supposed to be solving problems and making lives easier, but I've never met a group of people who complained more about their job or our customers than the team I'm on," says Jonah R., a customer service support worker. "It's not like this is what I want to be doing, but there's no point in making it worse for myself by wallowing."

"Why are you even showing up if you've already decided it's too hard or impossible?" asks Regina P., a retail associate. "Every shift, my manager acts so negative—we'll never make our numbers, we'll never beat last year's sales. It's boring and it's miserable."

More than one Curious Unicorn surveyed was in the nursing profession. They reported feeling undervalued and not finding joy in their work.

"Who in nursing or childcare or teaching or any other tradition-ally female job *is* appreciated enough?" asks nurse Anna W. "No one I know. Becoming a nurse seemed like the thing to do—all the women in my family were or are nurses, but I wish I'd taken more time to choose a path. I'm fine at nursing, but I don't love it. It's not my passion."

"I've worked with some incredibly inspiring women. They clearly love nursing, and I get why they find it fulfilling. It works for them. It does not work for me," says Kristy V.

### THE HAPPY-AT-WORK CHECKLIST

Have a Curious person on your hands? Here are some tips for managing them that will ensure everyone's peace and happiness. If you're a Curious person yourself, be sure to let your team know which of these tips work best for your work-ing style.

**Keep them interested.** Do this by monitoring their inter-est level on projects and people. You can help gauge where they are and maybe help or intervene before they get into a space where they aren't thriving.

**Help them if they begin to disengage.** If you notice a trend of disengagement, now is not the time to be hands off. Help find the source of what's causing your Curious person to retreat so you can find space where they can thrive, whether that's a perspective shift, a new project initiative, or a new role in the organization.

**Keep an eye on culture.** This is important to everyone, but Curious people feel it when culture is bad. Work to maintain a healthy culture on your team or in your company, and invite the Curious to help with that effort too. They're key players on your culture team.

**Use reality responsibly.** Sometimes you'll need to temper the optimism and wonder of a Curious person with a dose of reality. Be intentional with how you approach them, and always speak in a solution-oriented way to help them maintain their stability.

**Watch out for combos that don't work.** The Curious don't always get along with types like the Fast or the Productive. Watch for these and other people on your team and help your curious person navigate relationships so they don't get weighed down by them.

## JOBS THAT DO NOT WORK FOR THE CURIOUS

Curious people are remarkably resilient. You can make almost any subject interesting, and you can find value in even the most mundane tasks. But even you have your breaking point. We've found that these jobs do not work for Curious people:

- Data entry
- Assembly line worker
- Bookkeeper
- Tax accountant
- Insurance claims adjuster
- Mail carrier

## THINGS TO DO RIGHT NOW TO BE HAPPIER

If you're already in the workforce and you find yourself in a job that simply doesn't work for you or you're frustrated to be unemployed, don't despair. It will get better.

With the Curious, more than any other group, it's important to find a way out sooner rather than later. You have characteristics that make you incredibly successful when things are going right, but alas, if times be not fair, as the quote goes. It takes a while to get you down; Curious people are almost always optimists, after all. But once you're down, it's hard for you to find your spark again. The climb back to who you were before is a tough one.

Distress tolerance is the name of the game. Here's what will work best for Curious people like you.

### Learn something new

Your job might not be the least bit fulfilling right now, but you can live your best curious life in other ways. Learn something new. Socialize more, meet new people, or reconnect with old friends. Or take a deep dive into a subject you've always wondered about. Audit a class at a local college or find lectures online. Check out what speakers and exhibits your town's museums and libraries have going on. You never know where those things might lead you.

*Focus on what's right at work*

Toxic optimism is alive and well, and I don't want anyone to ignore their feelings. Feel your feelings at work. Be miserable, write scathing resignation letters in your head. But then, for the time being, try to think about the good things at work. You're there, doing a great job whether you like it or not, whether anyone likes you or not. You're doing your best and making a difference, however small. Maybe there are other good things about it, like the snack room or the printer. Whatever you need to hold on to, to stay your curious and good-natured self, use it.

## YOU'RE EQUAL TO THE TASK

You know yourself and what will help you be happy at work. Keep your chin up and your résumé updated. You'll find your happily ever after.

Say what you will about Jane Fonda, she may have made some bad choices in her personal life, but she was never unhappy in her career. So let's learn from this quote of hers: "Stay curious, keep learning, and keep growing. And always strive to be more interested than interesting."

## TAKEAWAYS

- You value spontaneity, solving problems, and socialization, but lots of people don't. Don't waste your time trying to fit in where you're not appreciated.
- Your ideal job has room for flexibility and autonomy plus the ability to work as a team. You'll be happy if you find a workplace with optimists and few, if any, gloomy sad sacks.

- It's really hard for curious people like you to get their spark back, so do your best not to lose it.

# CHAPTER 12

# CONNECTING WITH HAPPINESS

Connection, the ability to feel connected, is
neurobiologically wired. It's why we're here!

—Brené Brown

If you can connect people, you can create the future.

—Scott Heiferman

D o you love it when a plan comes together? So do the Connected.
At their best, the Connected are like Danny Ocean, fresh out
of prison (okay, maybe not that part) and ready to assemble a world-
class group of people to pull off a $160 million heist (maybe not that
part either). The point is, he knows whom to call for each role on
the team. He's got a pickpocket, an acrobat, an explosives expert,
mechanics, an electronics savant, and—maybe most important—a
best friend.

Being Connected is one of the best things you can do for yourself. Evolutionarily speaking, our hardwired need for connection helped early humans share resources and stay informed (and alive). Even today, it helps us to seek out relationships that enrich our lives and contribute to our overall well-being.

When you're Connected, you're the life of a party. Not because you're a genius with a cocktail shaker—though you are—or because you have the best taste in music—though you do—but because you know that if someone's not having a good time, you're not having a good time. Your empathy and ability to pick up on other people's energy is a blessing and a curse, but lucky for everyone you interact with, it's always a blessing for them.

As far as your career is concerned, it's just as beneficial. Being Connected allows you to build and maintain relationships with a variety of individuals in a variety of professions and positions. It's no different from having a diverse stock portfolio. Being Connected pays off.

You might be Connected if:

- You're an Enneagram type 3, 7, or 8 (as reported by 13, 14, and 8 percent, respectively, of the Connected).
- You're a high i in your DiSC assessment (38 percent of the Connected are high i).
- You're known as a "networker" and find it easy to keep in touch with everyone in your Rolodex (I'm dating myself, I know).
- You're responsive to others' needs.
- Authentic (28 percent of Connected people) and Purpose-Driven (33 percent) are your next highest Vander Index traits.

- Agile is your weakest Vander Index trait (only 9 percent of the Connected are high in Agile).
- You're an extrovert and have been described as a people person.
- English was your favorite subject in school (as reported by 23 percent).
- You ask good questions and genuinely care about the answers.

## MICRO TRAITS

Our happiest Connected Unicorns share two important micro traits. They're strategic, and they've got the memory of an elephant (or an equally robust system to make it seem like they do).

- **Strategic.** The Connected can network with anyone, but equally important is their ability to discern whom to connect with. Determining which leads are worth pursuing and which relationships are worth pouring into takes a level of strategy that others may not have.

  "I always ask myself how each new relationship can be mutually beneficial. It's not just about expanding my network but about creating meaningful partnerships that drive success for everyone involved," says Nicole L., a small-business owner.
- **Mind like a steel trap (or a good way to take notes).** The Connected know that having a good memory is invaluable when it comes to forging and maintaining meaningful relationships. It allows them to recall personal details, past conversations, and significant events, which in turn helps

to build trust and goodwill. This not only makes others feel valued and respected but also strengthens the bond over time.

"I always make it a point to remember key details about the people I interact with," says Sarah T., a senior marketing manager. "Whether it's their birthday, the name of their pet, or a major project they're working on, these small bits of information can go a long way in showing that you care and are truly invested in the relationship."

## THE HAPPIEST CONNECTED PERSON YOU KNOW:
## NIMA HASSAN

Nima Hassan is connected.

The Midwest is a far cry from the sunshine and heat of Somalia, but Hassan had a connection to Milwaukee, Wisconsin, so that's where she and her family moved when they were able to leave their Ethiopian refugee camp.

"I had an adopted sister there, so that's where they were able to place us," she says.

Hassan has always looked for—and found—connections between herself and others, even when it didn't seem possible.

"In Milwaukee, we were placed in a school with no other Somali kids," she says. "But we were all refugees. None of us spoke the same language. Even though we had to communicate through body language, I understood exactly what they were trying to say."

Soon after, Hassan's mother moved the family north, to Green Bay, in search of better schools for her children and a more stable Islamic community. Like so many children before her, Hassan had a terrible time in middle school.

"I was bullied by the other Somali kids," she says. "I hated it. I don't have good memories of middle school."

But in high school, things began to look up.

### Finding community

Hassan says that high school opened up lots of new opportunities. There, she found other Somali girls and quickly became part of a large group of friends.

"We all came from different camps in Ethiopia or Kenya, but we were all on the same journey," says Hassan. "I wasn't expecting to have as many friends whose experiences were so similar to mine."

With the confidence that being connected to her friends gave her, Hassan says she was able to start speaking up.

"We were encouraging and supporting each other and putting ourselves out there," she says. "In doing that, we were able to get accommodations for us to be able to pray during school, and we became quite well-known by our teachers and other students."

The group caught the attention of community advocates, including a woman named Katie Stockman, who was working in the schools as a social worker. Hassan says Stockman helped the girls see their potential and connected them with opportunities to write and create art, which was particularly fun for the girls because they didn't have a lot of opportunity to do art projects when they were younger.

"Katie and the others saw that we had a story to share with the nonrefugee community and motivated us to tell it," she says. "People were listening to us and were being super kind to us."

### Moving to Minnesota

Upon graduating from high school, Hassan thought she wanted to be a social worker like Katie or a nurse, which was the path her friends were taking. She enrolled in community college and started taking her gen eds, plus a few human anatomy classes.

"I passed the classes," she said. "But I was struggling. I decided the medical field was not for me."

Hassan and her family moved to Minnesota in 2018. She missed her friends but, she says, "We have internet and can stay connected."

She resumed her studies, this time with social work in mind. Hassan got her associate's degree and began working in a program with kids on the spectrum.

"I loved that job," she says.

Hassan had to take a break from the job when she had two babies in quick succession. But when she was able, Hassan went back into the workforce and back to school. She will graduate with her bachelor's in social work in May 2027.

For now, she is happily employed by a program called ARMHS (Adult Rehabilitation Mental Health Services) and is connecting clients with all the responses and opportunities at her disposal. It's very much a social worker–type job.

"I love my job," she says. "We do interventions and work with clients helping them with daily tasks, goal setting, and connect them with mental health facilities. I love, love my clients, and it doesn't feel like work anymore. They call me any time of the day, and I don't even mind. I'm happy to help."

### Nima Hassan's philosophy

Hassan has a knack for staying open to the people who come into her life, because you never know what connections might follow.

She says, "I tell people: You don't have control over who comes to your life, but you can be kind and invite the good people in. You can't expect everyone to be good, so you can't always be kind and inviting. You shouldn't have too many expectations. But when good people do come your way, recognize that and connect with them."

## WHAT HAPPINESS AT WORK LOOKS LIKE FOR YOU IF YOU'RE CONNECTED

The Connected thrive in work environments where they can leverage their strategic networking skills and strong memory to build meaningful relationships. The happiest Connected people have found satisfaction in jobs that allow them to connect with others, create mutually beneficial partnerships, and recall personal details that strengthen bonds. For them, happiness at work is deeply intertwined with the sense of fulfillment that comes from fostering genuine connections and making a positive impact on those around them.

Consider these careers if you're Connected:

- Publicist
- Sales associate
- Recruiter
- Community manager
- Lobbyist
- Politician
- Fundraiser
- Hairstylist
- Agent
- Entrepreneur
- Contractor

As with all the groups, the same six workplace happiness factors apply to the Connected.

*Having a good boss*

A good boss is crucial for a Connected person because it sets the tone for a positive and productive work environment. A good boss provides clear direction, support, and feedback, fostering a sense of trust and respect. And a good boss for a Connected person constantly looks for opportunities for their employees to network and make connections.

As Josie M., a community manager who loves her job, says, "Having a supportive boss who will always make me her plus one or sends me to networking events is one of the best parts of my job."

*Work-life balance*

Maintaining a balance between work and personal life is vital, especially for a Connected person, who rarely misses a networking opportunity. Being Connected often means attending events, meeting people, and forging relationships outside typical work hours, which can blur the lines between professional and personal time. But when managed well, this balance can create opportunities for work and your personal life.

As marketing associate Alex J. says, "Networking is a big part of my job and my passion. My company values work-life balance, so I never feel guilty about taking a day off after a long networking event. It keeps me fresh and motivated."

*Making enough money*

For the Connected, making enough money is a key element of job satisfaction, as it enables them to participate in various networking events and opportunities without financial stress. Feeling comfortably compensated helps the Connected invest in their professional relationships and personal growth.

As Jessica L., a successful sales manager, shares, "Getting paid well means I don't have to worry about expenses when attending industry conferences or networking dinners. It gives me the freedom to focus on building connections and advancing my career, which ultimately makes me happier and more motivated in my job."

## Autonomy and flexibility

Having autonomy and flexibility at work is essential for the Connected. When they feel as if they're trusted to manage their time and commitments themselves, they get a sense of freedom and trust, which goes a long way in workplace happiness. This, in turn, empowers them to attend networking events, meet new people, and build professional relationships without feeling constrained by rigid work schedules.

As Nathan B., a serial entrepreneur, told us, "The flexibility in my job gives me the liberty to explore new opportunities and expand my network."

## Professional growth

Connected people can't help it: They'll make their own professional growth happen. They'll seek out opportunities and occasionally even ask for permission before committing to them.

David H., a lobbyist, says, "I've been in rooms with high-level strategic leaders from the military, academia, business, and nonprofits. I realized what a great opportunity this was for me to learn necessary leadership skills simply by asking these men and women a simple question: What have you been learning lately? You wouldn't believe how much I learned by asking high-level leaders that simple question. Too often we are tempted to ask these types of leaders to help us do something to help with our agenda. I've found that learning from other leaders is much more important than getting something from them."

## Meaningful work

Going back to the evolutionary advantages of being connected, the Connected find meaning in their work when their ability to pull together types of information (whether that's people, information, or other knowledge) benefits their community.

Julia H., an organizer, says, "I'm not the one with the 'talent,' but I'm the one bringing it all together in a way that wouldn't be possible otherwise. I love being able to help in this way, and I feel it's really important."

---

"I would have followed you, my brother,

my captain, my king."

---

## WHERE THE CONNECTED LOSE THEIR WAY

Our least happy Connected Unicorns find themselves struggling in roles that demand prolonged isolation and repetitive tasks, such as those in technical writing, accounting, data entry, and similar professions. These roles can feel stifling and monotonous, devoid of the dynamic interaction and leadership opportunities that you as a connected person thrive on.

## Creating in a vacuum

Connected people need people. That's abundantly clear. So, when they're in jobs that have them working alone, they don't do their best.

Ryan D., a data entry specialist, tells us, "Working in data entry feels like I am trapped in a never-ending cycle of solitude and boredom. It's a constant struggle to stay motivated in this job."

## The definition of crazy

Connected people also struggle when the tasks at hand are monotonous. Their natural inclination to seek out meaningful connections and lead initiatives makes it pretty tough for them to remain engaged and satisfied in positions that do not leverage these strengths.

Sarah M., a web developer, says, "I dread going to work every day because it feels like I'm stuck in a loop of tedious tasks that drain my creativity and passion. Am I good at my job? Yes. Am I happy there? No."

---

**THE HAPPY-AT-WORK CHECKLIST**

Are you Connected? Do you manage a Connected person? Here are my top ways of successfully managing Connected people.

**Give them roles on your team to celebrate people or make people feel seen.** The Connected are the best at remembering personal details about the people around

---

them. Their teammate's dog's name? They know it. If you're celebrating someone's work anniversary, this is the person you want customizing the plan. If you need a pulse check on how someone is doing, this person can likely help.

**And make sure you know** *them.* They spend so much energy and brain space knowing so much about others— make sure they have a space with you to be known. Know how their family is doing, what trips they have planned, what they're most excited for this year. Anything that helps them feel known and seen goes a long way with the Connected.

**Help them balance the importance of connection and the importance of productivity.** Often, these things can war against each other, and the Connected Unicorn will always pick relationships when forced to choose. Help them know what situations they can lean into and which ones they should shift away from and prioritize the work.

**Oftentimes, Connected Unicorns find themselves in a career for which work-life balance is hard or they're work-ing unusual hours.** Make sure to check in on them regularly and that they're taking comp time to make up for the time spent doing the work. They also can have a hard time fully seeing how making connections is work, so double-check that they are honoring all the time they're investing and not just writing off some of it because it's fun for them.

**Let them manage their own calendar.** If you microman-age this type, it is a surefire way to shut them down. Make sure they have the flexibility and time needed to make the right connections in the right spaces.

**Figure out systems to help them manage their connec-tions.** Maybe that's a CRM system or even just a Google doc that lets them keep track of the connections they're making. But make sure to find a way to equip them to maintain those connections and allow your organization to leverage your connected resources for success.

## JOBS THAT DO NOT WORK FOR CONNECTORS

Isolation and repetitive tasks are not your friend. Avoid the freelance life. And if you're one of the 5 percent of people who are okay with full-time, in-office work, by all means, avoid remote work.[1] Here's a list of careers that aren't ideal for the Connected.

- Technical writer
- Accountant
- Data entry
- Editor
- Web developer
- Actuary
- Freelance writer

- Graphic designer
- Research scientist
- Artist
- Software developer
- Translator
- Photographer
- Archivist
- Technical support specialist
- Virtual assistant

## THINGS A CONNECTED PERSON CAN DO RIGHT NOW TO BE HAPPIER

If you're already in the workforce and you find yourself in a job that simply doesn't work for you or you're frustrated to be unemployed, don't despair. It will get better.

Here's my advice for distress tolerance in the meantime.

### Ask for help

I know, you're used to asking for favors for other people. That's the best part of being Connected. But it might be time to cash in some of that relational equity. Ask for any leads on opportunities that might suit you. You'll be surprised at how many people are willing to help.

### Pursue passion projects

If nothing can be done about work at the moment, look beyond it. Whether it's a hobby, a side hustle, or volunteering for a cause you care about, investing time in what you love can bring happiness that balances out your difficulties at work. Plus—and you know what I'm going to say here—these endeavors can lead to unexpected professional opportunities and personal growth. Life is what happens when you're making other plans. Sometimes, so are career opportunities.

## COUNT ON YOUR CONNECTIONS

As Tom Ford, a very Connected man, says, "The most important things in life are the connections you make with others."

You're charming, you're great with names, and you know a guy or gal for every job. Everyone in town knows your name. If you wanted to, you could successfully run for school board tomorrow. Don't let bad circumstances dim your light and the goodness that you bring to the world. Other people believe in you, and you should too.

## TAKEAWAYS

- Seek jobs that allow you to network and give you the flexibility to manage your own time.
- Avoid jobs that are monotonous or solitary.
- You have a vast wealth of resources simply because of your natural inclination to connect with people.

# CHAPTER 13

# WHAT'S NOT TO LIKE?
## FINDING HAPPINESS AT WORK
## WHEN YOU'RE LIKABLE

I like him. I really like him.

—Sancho Panza, on why he
gave up everything to follow Don Quixote

I was hiding under your porch
because I love you. Can I stay?

—Dug, the dog from *Up*

Anyone who was a child in the early aughts (or who parented one) knows Mo Willem's Pigeon books. Starting with not being allowed to drive the bus, our poor Pigeon hero faces a new form of adversity with every turn of the page. His foil, the Duckling, however, seems to live on a path of ease. When the Duckling gets a cookie, this almost sends the Pigeon over the edge. When he discovers that the Duckling got the cookie simply by "asking for it politely," the Pigeon is incredulous. "I ask for things all the time," he says. "I'm the asking-est pigeon in town."

Maybe it's because the Duckling's request for a cookie was a little more feasible than the Pigeon's wish to have a "hot dog party," or maybe it was the "politely" part of the ask. The Duckling is more Likable to the powers that be and comes out on top because of it.

You might be Likable if:

- You're an Enneagram type 7 or 9 (15 and 13 percent of the Likable are).
- You're a high i on the DiSC assessment scale, along with 38 percent of your Likable peers).
- You're a social butterfly.
- High school wasn't as bad for you as other people say it was for them.
- People generally agree with you.
- You've been in more than five weddings as a bridesmaid or a groomsman.
- You find you "win" things more often than most.
- Your next strongest Vander Index traits are Authentic (29 percent) and Solver (27 percent).
- Your weakest Vander Index trait is Fast (only 10 percent are strong in Fast).
- Your favorite subject in school was art, band, or other fine arts (26 percent of the Likable love the arts).

## MICRO TRAITS OF THE LIKABLE

Our happiest Likable Unicorns shared three key micro traits. They're:

- **Thoughtful.** You can't be Likable if you're not thinking, especially about others. "I discovered that when I talked less and listened to people, they talked more and began to trust me. I work hard to be thoughtful of how I am being received in the moment and adjust when needed. I pay attention to the details people share with me and remember them. It makes people feel valued," says Seth O., a city councilman.

- **Inquisitive.** Most people like talking about themselves. Ask them questions, and you're off and running. "Some of the best impressions I've ever made, some of the most successful interviews I've ever had, have been the result of me doing nothing but asking questions of the person I was with. Somehow, me asking about their families and interests translated into me being exceedingly qualified for the job at hand. Being likable makes life a lot easier," says Brenda A., a director of donor engagement.

- **Outgoing.** You can be Likable as an introvert, but you get a lot further when you're an extrovert, sharing your warmth and geniality to any and all. Sarah J., a retail manager, says, "Whether I'm at church, work, the hair salon, my kids' school, whatever, I genuinely want to make connections with people. First, I look for an 'in' to start a conversation. This could be the sports team on their hat or something I hear them talking to someone else about. Then I make it known, in some fashion, that I want to talk with them. Once the conversation begins, I genuinely take interest in their thoughts and do all that I can to make them feel like they're the most important person in the room to me. Because, unless my husband or kids are standing next to me, they really are. Living for moments like these—where I make a genuine connection with someone because I care—has made me more effective in work and in life."

## THE HAPPIEST LIKABLE PERSON YOU KNOW: ROSS MOLLET

If you catch more flies with honey, consider Ross Mollet the ultimate flycatcher.

Currently the creative director for a multinational kitchen and bath manufacturer, Mollet says, "Other people can do the job and come up with ideas as effectively as I can, but they might not be as enjoyable to work with."

Mollet has learned, for reasons both selfish and altruistic, that being likable is one of the best characteristics you can have if you want to be happy at work.

### Not always "a joy to have in class"

Growing up in Oconomowoc, Wisconsin, Mollet says he wasn't always everyone's cup of tea. "I was a troublemaker," he says. "I'd ask stupid questions in class, shout out answers without being called on."

But even as he was trying his teachers' patience, something about Mollet was likable enough to warrant a little special treatment. "My third-grade teacher, Mrs. Lobbs, made a deal with me that for every day I didn't get my name on the board, I'd get a sticker. If I filled out a whole sheet of stickers, she'd take me to Burger King for lunch," he says.

Mollet is the only child of parents who were both in sales. He didn't know what exactly he wanted to be when he grew up, but he was learning firsthand what it takes to be successful.

"Anytime you're winning people over to your ideas, it's sales," he says. "And sales is the transfer of enthusiasm from one person to another. It's a lot easier to do this when you're likable."

A bit of showmanship doesn't hurt, either, and Mollet rivals P. T. Barnum in this department. "All my life, I've liked telling stories and coming up with ideas," he says. "Science fairs, book reports, whatever, I've always loved to present ideas. I couldn't wait for the next opportunity to stand in front of people and get them excited about what I was excited about."

Majoring in marketing at the University of Wisconsin–Oshkosh seemed like the natural next step for Mollet. But it turned out that a marketing degree came with class requirements like financial accounting, statistics, and calculus. These were not for him. There were no presentations in these classes, no opportunities to get a crowd excited about anything.

"I did really poorly in those classes," he says. "But then someone told me you could enroll in the college of journalism and specialize in advertising and public relations." Mollet did just that and began to thrive.

"I had classes like speech and communications and English literature," he says. "Those were much more my style."

**The process is the job . . . and the process may as well be fun**

After graduation, Mollet headed for warmer climes and started work at an advertising firm in Florida. There, he met Papa John, worked on campaigns for Nissan, and got a sense of what worked and what didn't for him in terms of career happiness.

"When your job is to come up with ideas and then sell the client on those ideas, you're rarely working in a vacuum," he says. "You're collaborating with people. And when that's the case, it really helps to be the guy people want to collaborate with."

Mollet soon discovered that talent alone wasn't enough to get you selected for the interesting projects.

"In the agency or creative environment, projects are offered to the people who are likable," he says. "The people who have control over who gets selected for a project ask themselves, *Who do I want to trudge through this process with?*

*That sad sack, negative guy? Or Ross?* Being likable gets you opportunities that you don't get with talent alone."

"Plus," says Mollet. "You can't be creative when there's tension among your team. It just makes the job harder. I try to be as likable as possible to make people feel as comfortable as possible. That might sound like I'm trying to be a people pleaser, but selfishly, I want the people I work with to be happy to make it better for me."

### Likable all the way to the top

After climbing as high as he could go in an agency setting, Mollet took his talents to an in-house opportunity in Kohler, Wisconsin. Although the years had taken his hair and youth, he remains as likable as ever, as enthusiastic about sharing ideas as he was for his first elementary school science fair.

And, as always, rejection, when it comes, does not get Mollet down. He remains likable.

"I rarely present ideas that I'm not genuinely excited about," he says. "But my career isn't defined by one idea. I have literally hundreds of opportunities a year to nail it. It's like baseball. The guy that strikes out a lot? Well, he also hits a lot of home runs. If one of my ideas doesn't land, it's not that big of a deal. I'm rarely presenting just one idea, and if you don't like those, give me a day and I'll come up with five more."

Staying positive and, as a result, likable is easy for Mollet. "I try to stay in the present. I don't dwell too much on the past. In college, I loved the fact that if I didn't love a class, it was only a semester. I love that, in my work, projects never last more than three to six months. I would get bored otherwise, and for me to be my best, I need to stay focused and present."

Mollet's advice is to consciously and intentionally work on your likability. One way to do this is to present your most winning self. For this reason, he says he always goes on camera in meetings. It's a valuable chance to convey his likability through his face and expressions.

Another way to become the likable person at your job, he says, is to pay attention to the little projects: "You work on these big, long projects, but in between there's little problems to solve, and when they arise, people go to the person who is a joy to work with. Yeah, it's more work, but those 'Can you help me with this?' one-off projects help get you further in your career. Do that and the big guys will notice you."

**Likability beyond the workplace**
"For sure being likable has helped me personally," says Mollet. "It's gotten me out of jams, gotten me upgraded in

hotels and on flights. I find that if you're very polite and ask, it usually works out."

## WHAT HAPPINESS AT WORK LOOKS LIKE FOR YOU IF YOU'RE LIKABLE

Almost everyone appreciates a dog who is happy to see them, who makes it feel like they're the only person alive who could possibly be the source of this much joy. That's what the Likable are like.

If you're Likable, you know that the effort you make toward others will come back around for your own benefit. As such, you need a job that will allow for some kind of transaction. You need to be your Likable self, and you need a way for that likability to shine back on you in some way.

The most successful Likable Unicorns know they've been gifted with the ability to make others feel like the best version of themselves, and they use their gift freely. The Likable know that you don't have to be talented, smart, or particularly good. As long as you make people feel special, you'll be likable, which is way better.

Likable Unicorn and administrator Dorin C. puts it like this: "Bottom line: The only thing someone will remember about you is how you make him feel."

## THE JOB FOR YOU

The happiest Likable Unicorns have jobs that require working as a team, preferably in-person or hybrid, some type of sales aspect, and an opportunity to be appreciated.

Likable designer Kristie K. says this about her job: "I believe my personality allows me to naturally give support, cooperate, be a good listener, and be a good team player at work. Many people gravitate toward that and the sense of stability and sincere appreciation that I can give. I really like collaboration because it allows me to hear all ideas, give feedback, and make decisions together. I also have i (influence) personality traits, which bring in encouraging others, friendly relationships, and optimism. My team and I function really well, and I love going to work in the morning."

Consider these careers if you're Likable:

- Creative director
- Interior designer
- Real estate agent
- Sales director
- Buyer/purchaser
- Life coach
- Banking/investing
- Flight attendant
- Consulting
- Personal shopper
- Motivational coach
- Tour guide
- Entrepreneur

As with all the groups, the same six workplace happiness factors apply to the Likable.

## Having a good boss

A Likable person can work for a grinchy boss, but it's not easy . . . for the boss. If you're Likable, it won't really matter who your boss is as long as someone of authority is noticing your winning ways. But when it's just you and a bad boss, and your proverbial light is hidden under their grumpy bushel, it's not ideal.

Amy K., a bank vice president, says she learned likability from her boss: "My first job at a credit union, I had an amazing mentor who took the time to praise me when I was doing something right but to also discipline me when I was lacking. He really poured into me as I showed interest and enthusiasm for learning and moving up the corporate ladder. By the end of my five years at the bank, I had secured an assistant branch manager position and was well-liked by everyone I worked with. As I am now taking on a new role, I continue to use a lot of what my boss and mentor taught me in my first job. He was an awesome leader who really took the time to get to know his employees and pour into each of them. He was full of integrity, and it showed in everything he did. I think listening and connecting with people goes a long way; people want to be seen and heard. I am blessed that such a great leader was put into my path."

## Work-life balance

Likable people who are happy at work generally have an easier time than most achieving work-life balance. This is because our most successful Likable Unicorns seem to have very little problem with boundaries. They simply say what they need to say, with love and kindness, and their boundaries are generally respected. They're also emotionally intelligent enough to know what's going to drain them or cause burnout.

"I find if I am clear with what I need right at the outset, expectations are managed and everyone wins," says Bert F., a housewares buyer.

## Making enough money

Likable people are often kept on staff even if they're not 100 percent necessary. If you're Likable, you may well be the personality hire. And that's a pretty great position to be in. As *Forbes* writer Jack Kelly says, "Vibes-based hiring captures workplace cultural values starting to supersede skills requirements. . . . It highlights the importance of the work environment. Skills can be taught, but likability and personality fit may be more challenging to instill later."[1]

And when your supervisors see the value you bring to the job, you should be getting paid well enough for it.

## Autonomy and flexibility

If you're Likable, you need enough autonomy and flexibility to meet the needs of your personal life, but when you're at work, it's helpful for you to have goals and key performance indicators. Otherwise, you might just spend the whole time being the office's social butterfly, which isn't the worst thing, but you'll be more successful with some guardrails.

"If I didn't make a to-do list at the start of my day and block off time in my calendar to focus on the tasks at hand, I'd probably end up spending the whole day asking people how their families are or listening to their latest challenges," says Kathleen L., a legal assistant. "I'm really genuinely interested in my colleagues, and I want them to be happy. I can't help it!"

## Professional growth

The Likable are usually the first to get the opportunity to go on that boondoggle or fly to Cabo for a training seminar. Because you're likable, your supervisors assume your interest in wanting to grow professionally. It's a great way to get ahead and develop in your career.

"People know I'm good to travel with, I like to learn, and that I'll take development opportunities seriously," says Devin S., an HR generalist.

On the other hand, feeling stuck in a role without chances for advancement can be incredibly frustrating for you if you're Likable. You tend to have high aspirations, so if your career feels like it's going nowhere, you can get dissatisfied fast.

## Meaningful work

Likable people find happiness in roles where their genuine interest in others and positivity are put to good use. Our happiest Likable Unicorns use their interpersonal skills on a daily basis to help create a joyful work environment for themselves and others.

"Early on in my leadership experience I learned that people won't go along with you if they can't get along with you," says clinic administrator Jeff J. "Coupled with my natural love for and value of people, I've been able to really grow as a leader and build solid meaningful relationships. It's been the most rewarding part of my career and what's brought me the most happiness."

"Why don't you like me? Why don't you
like me, without making me try?"

## WHERE LIKABLE PEOPLE STRUGGLE

Even the most Likable person at work can get frustrated when
they're not in the right role or office culture isn't optimal.

### Too much or too little management

Our happiest Likable Unicorns value their independence and creativity. Working in parallel with colleagues rather than under the
scrutiny of a micromanager is the best balance for the Likable. At
the same time, if their efforts go unnoticed or the Likable person is
left alone for too long, they will get demoralized and demotivated.
Likable people need recognition to be at their best.

### Dysfunctional dynamics

Likable people are happy to go along with most of what goes on in
the office. They know everyone's personality is different, and they
give a lot of grace. This is all part of why they're so likable to begin
with. But even the Likable have their limits. Some deal-breakers
we've heard from our least happy Likable Unicorns are:

- **Injustice.** Likable people become miserable people when
  they feel taken advantage of just because they're usually
  so easygoing and chill, or if they're denied opportunities
  because they're not the squeaky wheel.

- **Bad communication.** Likable people want to do a good job. If they're not communicated with effectively, they get frustrated.
- **Drama.** Being the peacemaker and navigating various personalities looks easy for the Likable, but it can drain them of their bonhomie over time.

## THE HAPPY-AT-WORK CHECKLIST

Have a Likable person on your hands? Are you yourself Likable? Here are some tips for managing them that will help everyone stay happy. And likable.

**Help them manage their time.** This type is someone that everyone wants to be around and spend time with, which is great! But it can also be hard for them to say that they need to finish something. If possible, give this person an office or space with a door so that when they need uninterrupted space to get things done, they can have it easily.

**Give them opportunities to partner with other people.** Any opportunity to collaborate with others and contribute to a team will be a bright spot in their day.

**Celebrate their wins.** If there's something they've done well or a success resulted from their work, make sure they know that you noticed and celebrate it widely.

**Build a strong relationship with the Likable.** They are pouring into others and putting effort into people. They are often the people who put effort into maintaining relation-ships. Make sure you do the same with them.

**Make sure you're holding them accountable to their work.** Sometimes a Likable Unicorn has depended on their likability enough that they can get by with the minimum requirements for their work. Make sure they are still chal-lenged in their role and held accountable to their work so they can be successful in all aspects.

**One of the best ways to hold them accountable is to help them establish boundaries.** Give them freedom to draw them where they will, but also help them set boundaries when it doesn't come naturally to them.

**Make sure they know they're going somewhere.** While connections and relationships are absolutely vital, the Likable Unicorn needs to know that they are working toward a goal or a growth milestone. Help them see their progress, too, as they work toward this.

**Walk with them if they are experiencing something or someone frustrating them.** The Likable Unicorn thrives when things are joyous and happy, but life is not always that way. When it's not all sunshine and roses, make sure to create time for them in those moments and help them move through that.

> **Give them spaces to influence company culture.** If your
> company has a task force or a culture team or opportunities
> to weigh in, in this area, look to the Likable Unicorns.

## THINGS TO DO RIGHT NOW TO BE HAPPIER

As a Likable person, you have a naturally positive attitude that is the result of a tremendous amount of resilience. But even you need some extra bolstering from time to time. If things aren't ideal now, give these tactics a chance.

### *Recharge with friends and family*

Go where you're most valued to feel better about yourself, your career prospects, and everything else. Likable people need to be reminded of how important they truly are to those who know them best.

### *Call in favors*

People like you! If you haven't thought of it yet, it's time to scroll through your contacts and reach out to someone who might be able to help. They don't know you're miserable, and they don't have to. Use your genuine interest in others to connect and your curiosity to ask for and find something better. Watch: They'll be happy to help someone who's always been so helpful to them.

*Practice self-care*

When you're being likable to others, you can sometimes forget to like yourself. Take a bath, get a massage, go to a yoga class, get a blowout, get a shoeshine, take a hike, or do anything else that helps you feel happier about your wonderful self.

*Accept that you're not always going to be everyone's cup of tea*

My family and I love the show *Emily in Paris*. I think it does a terrific job of illustrating some big differences between French and American culture. One major theme is Emily's very American need to be liked. Sometimes she's able to skate through on her charm and good intentions, and other times, she's too much to deal with for the cool, calm French, particularly her friend/rival Camille.

"Leave me alone, you illiterate sociopath," Camille writes to Emily.

Like Emily, you may need to come to terms with not being universally liked. When you do, you'll be happier.

## NEVER FALL OUT OF LOVE WITH YOURSELF

You've got charm and you've got grace. You know what works for you and where your pain points are. Don't wait to find a job that will tick all your happiness boxes. As Emily says, "Life's too short to be stuck in a job you hate. Do something that makes you happy."

## TAKEAWAYS

- You value connection, collaboration, and the positive reinforcement that comes from helping people. You'll be happy when your job encompasses these elements.
- Likable people like you are well-equipped to deal with office drama and keep the peace, but be careful to not let it exhaust you. Find the right balance of being likable for your own sake as well as for the sake of others.
- Even when you're as likable as you are, there's always going to be some misguided person who isn't your biggest fan. Keep going.

# CHAPTER 14

# TAKING CARE
# OF BUSINESS
## PRODUCTIVE HAPPINESS

I love the challenge of starting at zero every day and
seeing how much I can accomplish.

—Martha Stewart

Well, isn't that a stupid knife.

—also Martha Stewart

Taking on projects big and small and getting them done—and done well—isn't easy, but if it were, would it be worth it? If this sounds like you, you're probably Productive. You might have Productive tendencies if:

- You're an Enneagram type 3 (20 percent) or 1 (17 percent of the Productive).

- You're a high D (29 percent) or C (27 percent of Productive people) on the DiSC assessment scale.
- You love competition, but more than that, you love winning.
- Your principles are your guardrails.
- You get annoyed by laziness, whether it's in the way your server brings you your salad or the state of your hotel room's towels—it's not that hard to fold a piece of terry cloth into a swan.
- If it's worth doing, it's worth doing well.
- You find peace in order.
- Mess stresses you out.
- Your next strongest Vander Index traits are Purpose-Driven and Prepared, with 39 and 28 percent of the Productive reporting, respectively.
- Your weakest Vander Index trait is Anticipator, with only 9 percent scoring high in this strength.
- You're one of the 26 percent of your fellow Productive people who loved history in school.

## MICRO TRAITS OF THE PRODUCTIVE

Our happiest Productive Unicorns reported three traits, over and over again. They are:

- **Perfectionism.** Not all perfectionists are Productive, but many Productive people are perfectionists. They just can't help themselves. The successful ones have learned how to manage their perfectionism. Quality analyst Tessa B. says, "I am very productive because I feel responsible for outcomes. This, however, shows the shadow side to my strength: perfectionism. Learning to be more self-aware and establish better boundaries with my time has helped me keep perfectionism in check."

- **Drive.** Whether intrinsic or extrinsic motivation is at work, Productive people feel the need to produce. Restaurant manager Richard B. says, "I am productive because as I was growing up, with a family of ten total siblings, I always felt that I had to produce for my parents to 'see' me. The trait or desire to be noticed is a blessing, but it can also be abused. I was only a crew person for my first three years, and the next seventeen years at the restaurant, I was in leadership roles. I always push myself to go above and beyond. The inward strive to be the best allowed me to be noticed."

- **Organization.** Picasso was incredibly Productive, one of the most prolific artists in Western art history. This was thanks to a routine he rarely diverted from: breakfast and socializing from waking up at 11:00 a.m. until about 2:00 p.m. Then, painting until taking a break to eat at 10:00 p.m., then, more painting, usually until around 3:00 a.m. Most of our Productive Unicorns don't have the luxury of keeping teenager hours, but they do recognize the importance of routine. Melissa B., an event coordinator, says, "I am ultra organized, fast paced, and able to multitask and do the administrative as well as the physical things needed. I get better at this by maintaining a routine and delegating less complicated tasks to others."

## THE HAPPIEST PRODUCTIVE PERSON YOU KNOW:
### BENJAMIN DREYER

For people who can't tolerate imperfection, who see errors and feel compelled to fix them, the world can be a frustrating place. That's when, says Benjamin Dreyer, "You have to take your crazy and turn it into a virtue."

Dreyer is the recently retired copy chief and managing editor of the Random House imprint of the Penguin Random House publishing group. You may know him better as the bestselling author of *Dreyer's English: An Utterly Correct Guide to Clarity and Style*. Or you might follow him, now that he's abandoned X like so many others, on Bluesky as a leading language guru of that platform. He's taken his crazy and not only made it a virtue but made it an art. And a successful, happy career.

### A good eye and a good ear
A New York native, Dreyer graduated from Northwestern University in 1979 and eventually returned to Manhattan, not entirely sure of his path.

"I'd spent most of my twenties working in restaurants and bars and going to double features, going to the zoo," he says. "A lovely life if you're a child."

Dreyer says he didn't know what to do for a career, but he talked to an author friend who suggested he might be a good proofreader. The friend would give him bound galleys (a proof copy of a manuscript that's bound like a book), and every now and then, he says, he'd point out "with great respect and care" the errors he found.

It turns out Dreyer had "a good eye and a good ear," which made him especially suited for proofreading work. He connected with a production editor at St. Martin's Press, who began giving him freelance work.

"I had no formal training, and to be honest, my knowledge of the English language was really on the spotty side," says Dreyer, whose skill at this point was mostly instinctive. "It behooved me to learn what I was doing."

Dreyer started reading style manuals and learning the why behind the rules of English.

"Learn it all so that you know what you're talking about," he says. "Learn the jargon so you can know it." But in practice, says Dreyer, you don't need to use the jargon or cite the rules. You just need to know what's right. As he learned more and bolstered his credibility, Dreyer graduated himself from freelance proofreader to freelance copy editor, a position with more room for creativity and involvement with the formation of a book. He became part of the conversation that goes on in the margins of manuscripts as they make their way through production.

## The (necessary) boundaries of a nine-to-five job

Dreyer liked the freelance life, but the lack of boundaries sometimes made it a challenge for a person with "a neurotic compulsion to make everything right." He found that he'd occasionally find himself at three in the morning trying to finish a project because he bit off more than he could chew.

A production editor position came up at Random House, Dreyer took it, and the rest is history. Dreyer ended up working there for thirty years, rising in the ranks from production editor to copy chief and managing editor.

"I loved the books; I loved the words. I had the obsessive need to make things perfect, but also it was wonderful fun to work with the authors," Dreyer says.

"Working with these people, it was just a complete dream," Dreyer says. He recalls his mother reading *Nicholas and Alexandra* by Robert Massie when he was little; decades later, he got to work on Massie's books. It was the same with Peter Straub. Dreyer says in college he ran to the bookstore to buy *Ghost Story* when it came out. And then, years later, he was working on Straub's books.

"The deal always was, if the author liked you and you liked the author, you got to keep working with them. It's a lovely continuity," he says.

Of course, when you're productive and a perfectionist like Dreyer, the highs of working with the best of the best can be offset by the lows of making a mistake. Other types of people would forgive themselves more easily, but then other types of people wouldn't be good proofreaders.

"Early in my career, I had left one tiny misspelling in a book. I remember sitting in my office with the door closed and sulking," he says. Dreyer was able to move on, eventually.

### Why the work worked

"The job was great for me because it was, on the whole, something that I'm very good at and like to do," says Dreyer. But he also points out that the variety of the work was essential to his happiness. "It's always a new book, often a new author who is great and you get to be friends," he says.

But the shadow side of the "doing what you're good at and thus being happy" equation is the list of things you can't do. For Dreyer, it's his "intolerance of error and my inability to leave anything alone that isn't right."

"Your strengths are your weaknesses; your weaknesses are your strengths. I was able to translate that into being extremely good at what I did," he says. Dreyer says his job helped him channel his need to fix things in a positive way. "It opened up the pressure valve," he says. "All that steam that builds up in you has a place to go."

**Being open to chance**

Dreyer is a rare modern example of a person who didn't job-hop to get to the top. "I don't necessarily rock my own boat, so I wasn't paying attention to see if someone else was looking for a copy chief. Other people have different approaches, and some people are more ambitious than I was," he says.

He stayed and experienced what he calls "the natural evolution of doing work and being good at it." Dreyer became copy chief and managing editor and had to stop working on books.

"There was no way to bring focus to a single book when you're running a whole department," he says. "It was a readjustment in my life."

When Susan Kamil, his Random House editor in chief, asked Dreyer to copyedit Elizabeth Strout's new book *The Burgess Boys*, because she'd specifically requested him, he was eager to do so. This led to the creation of Dreyer's own book, *Dreyer's English*, a collection of everything a person needs to know about writing style.

Dreyer says in the past he'd thought for "maybe two and a half seconds" about writing a copyediting book. Inspired by his work with Strout, he was newly consumed with the idea, and he was compelled to write it.

"I managed to spend thirty years doing the thing that I loved, being quite content with my job. But then I saw the possibility of doing other things while having this lovely safety net for myself," he says.

### Dreyer's advice

Being happy, says Dreyer, is a combination of finding the things that you like and doing them but also leaving the door and your brain open to follow whatever luck, chance, and serendipity comes along.

"I was blessed with the right opportunities being made manifest to me, with making a lot of good choices, with getting to all the right places, with finding something I was good at. And I loved it all," he says.

"There were books that were difficult and schedules that were impossible," Dreyer says. "I wouldn't want anybody to think that all I ever had was fun, but I loved my job, and it meant everything to me. I always wanted to do it really well, and I can safely and happily say that by the time it was time for me to retire, maybe it was getting a little old."

For aspiring proofreaders, Dreyer has this advice: "If you take all of those perfectionist qualities and add love of literature, love of publishing and books, it's a nice way to make a living. And if you want to do a job that's fulfilling and, on

WORK HOW YOU ARE WIRED

many levels, enjoyable, you could do worse than decide to
be a proofreader or copy editor."

For him, Dreyer says, "It worked out nicely."

## WHAT HAPPINESS AT WORK LOOKS LIKE FOR YOU IF YOU'RE PRODUCTIVE

The Productive are the show dogs of our worker types. But they're not just any show dogs; they've got style *and* substance. Think: a Newfoundland diving into Canadian waters to save a man who'd fallen overboard; Bernese mountain dogs acting as slightly smaller Clydesdales hauling many times their weight; huskies pulling mushers and lifesaving vaccines across Alaska. These dogs are stunning, but they're also workers.

As much effort as Productive Unicorns make to fit the model for what they should look like on the outside, they have brains that work even harder. It's not just enough to look good; they have to *be* good too. What's more, they have to produce products, outcomes, or performances that they're proud of because, otherwise, what's the point?

So, whether they're catering a home wedding for two hundred, counting the till at the end of the night, or detailing a hot rod, you'll never find the Productive leaving well enough alone. Because to them, there is no such thing as "well enough."

Productive people thrive in jobs where there are clear objectives. When you know what the assignment is, you can figure out how to execute it perfectly. Unlike the more data-focused Unicorn types, the Productive don't need quantitative key performance indicators to live up to. Qualitative factors are just as important.

If you're Productive, you have no problem starting at the bottom. You know you won't be there long. And once you're in charge, buckle up.

## THE JOB FOR YOU

In our survey, the happiest Productive people have jobs that require exacting standards, personal accountability, a little bit of fearlessness, and a high level of autonomy.

Consider these careers if you're Productive:

- Attorney
- Project manager
- Surgeon
- Business owner
- Architect
- Landscaper
- Consultant
- Investment banker
- Interpreter
- Chef
- Copy editor

As with all the groups, the same six workplace happiness factors apply to the Productive.

### *Having a good boss*

A Productive person will thrive under a boss who shares their need for order and organization and their love of high expectations. You demand excellence from yourself and will expect even more from a so-called superior.

"I want to be my boss when I grow up," says executive assistant Sarah V. "She's a perfect example of #goals. She sees potential in me that I didn't know was there, and I know she has my best interests at heart because we think the same."

## Work-life balance

It's hard for a Productive person to leave when the job isn't yet complete, so work-life balance is a challenge. Your life is made easier, however, when you know you have enough time to get your tasks right. You can't help wanting to do the job well, so a workplace that can accommodate your need for perfection without putting you in the position of staying late or spending too much of your own free time will help keep you happier and balanced—whether you like it or not.

"It's sometimes frustrating, but because I'm allotted a certain number of hours in the project management system, I know that it's not good for me or my company to take too long on any one task. There's a point of diminishing returns," says production artist Mark G.

## Making enough money

Productive people are competitive, so there's a very good chance you know what everyone in the department is making. You need to know you're being paid fairly and what you're worth. And you need to be paid on time.

"I worked at a start-up once," says financial planner Erin C. "It was extremely nerve-racking because we never knew if we were going to make payroll that week. I know some people get a thrill out of unpredictability, but those were incredibly stressful times for me."

## Autonomy and flexibility

The Productive need clear direction and expectations, but then, you need everyone to get out of the way. You're resourceful, strong willed, and self-reliant, so you'll do just fine without anyone else interfering. Plus, you don't love others trying to influence you; it's a win-win when you're left to your own devices.

"The absolute worst thing you can do when I'm working is to come in at the last minute with suggestions for how things should be changed," says architect Ted E. "I promise you your suggestions are not better than what I've got going."

## Professional growth

Knowing there's a clear path to the top and knowing the steps you'll need to take to get there is important to a Productive person. Almost as important is being recognized along the way. Your commitment to high standards is a big part of your ego, so a little celebration for you now and then wouldn't go amiss.

"I'm a words of affirmation person to begin with," says Britney B., a project manager. "So getting a little treat in the form of public recognition while I'm on the way up in my career is extra rewarding."

## Meaningful work

The Productive find meaning and purpose in their work when they can see how their high standards and demand for excellence translate to successful outcomes.

Danielle H. says it was an easy decision for her to become a surgeon for this reason. "When I'm at my best, people live," she says. "There's a direct correlation between what I bring to my work and my success. I would want someone exactly like me operating on me or my loved ones."

"That sweater is not just blue.
It's not turquoise. It's not lapis.
It's actually cerulean."

## WHERE PRODUCTIVE PEOPLE STRUGGLE

That quote from *The Devil Wears Prada* reflects the frustration Productive people feel when they're not in the right working circumstances. Of course, since this quote was from the boss herself, Meryl Streep's Miranda Priestly, her particular brand of productive was going to navigate the workplace—her workplace—just fine. But in our research, we've seen over and over how being surrounded by people who don't share your same values is kryptonite to Productive people.

## SOMETIMES THE ISSUE IS SIMPLY THAT THEIR CEILING IS YOUR FLOOR

We've heard from a lot of Productive people who are unhappy in their jobs. In fact, they're the group with the largest percentage of people who are unhappy in their jobs. I suspect this is because, more than any other group, the Productive can be as sensitive as they are committed to getting things right. You don't shy away from confrontation, but it takes a toll. The hardest things for productive people to deal with at work are lack of support for their methods and standards, disregard for their opinions, and an overall feeling of not being valued.

"It's really frustrating because I see so many areas for improvement at my workplace," says Stephen V., a manufacturing director. "There's a lot of low-hanging fruit. Simple little changes that would make a big difference, but management is slow, and there's so much bureaucracy that positive change never happens."

"I'm not sorry that I have high standards," says project manager Michelle N. "I'm sorry my boss doesn't."

"It's like there's a train coming and I can see it, so I tell my team, 'Hey, there's a train coming and it's about to hit us,' and they ignore me," says salesperson Brian K. "There's only so many times I can be right about something I told them would happen before I start looking for a better job."

"When your immaculately curated presentation gets the same acknowledgment as the one Diana just threw together fifteen minutes before the meeting, it's demoralizing," says Hannah F., an education specialist.

## THE HAPPY-AT-WORK CHECKLIST

Have a Productive person on your hands? Here are some tips for managing them that will help everyone thrive even while living up to their exacting standards. And if you *are a* Productive person, see which of these resonates with you best.

**Encourage when things are going well!** A behavior or performance win will be repeated if it's praised.

**Be forgiving with one-off mistakes but address trends.** This is a leadership principle I live by, but it's especially important for Productive people. If they are also a perfectionist (likely, as we've seen), you want to create a safe space for them to admit when they've made a mistake so you can work through it with them. This will help them learn and grow from it rather than send them down their usual shame spiral.

**Help them process constructive feedback.** This type has an especially hard time processing things they need to improve on, especially if they haven't noticed it in themselves yet. When addressing issues or giving constructive feedback, always be neutral and lay out a path forward to improve so they can run at the improvement action or plan.

**Lead with the why.** It's hard to get a Productive person on board with a plan they didn't create or approve of, and often this type doesn't get final say or get to have input. Walk them through the why of whatever it is you're working on—a project, task, team or company goal—so they can process it and get on board more easily. Additionally, when this type loses sight of the why, that is when they are most likely to spiral. Watch for the early warning signs and talk early and often about why you're doing something or the purpose behind it.

**Help them manage their time.** Productive people will work forever and burn themselves out. And they will also take way more time than needed on a project because they are trying to live up to their own impossible standards. Help them see when good is needed versus when perfect is needed. A good way to do this is to give bite-sized deadlines, and base things on time and not quality. They will hold themselves to quality; you as a manager need to hold them to time.

**Keep them based in reality.** Watch the narratives they are telling themselves and help them see truth, good or bad. When this type spirals, it's often due to a false narrative that they've created in their mind (*I'm not good enough, I haven't hit X metric so I'm bad at my job, I'm not as talented as this other person*). Make sure they're seeing clearly and not telling themselves things that aren't true.

**Set clear goals but don't micromanage.** Clarity is so important to Productive people, but giving them space to run with it and mixing in availability and support when they need it is what helps them thrive.

**Help them give others grace.** Productive people can get a bit judgy with other people; have you noticed? It's the fastest way to become discontented with a job and a team, and it makes them a bad teammate too.

**Remind them to use their powers for good.** Let's not kid ourselves: Most villains are Productive perfectionists. We need to keep yours on the side of good. This is where we've seen Productive people falter and get in their own way. They go down a thought process that ultimately becomes a spiral and then speak out of turn, offend leadership, or meddle where they aren't meant to. Use the rather outrageous phrasing of "good versus evil," if it's helpful, to have a common language and make for a good shorthand for "think about if what you're planning to do, say, or think is really such a good idea."

## JOBS THAT DO NOT WORK FOR THE PRODUCTIVE

For better or worse, your ego is attached to your productivity. If you can't quantify your productivity in your job, it's probably not the job for you. Our least happy Productive Unicorns have jobs that are included here:

- Fire tower lookout observer
- Mid-level government position
- Casino dealer
- Compliance officer
- Insurance member services rep
- Insurance claims adjuster

- Basically anything to do with insurance
- Real estate appraiser
- Office manager
- Astrologer

## THINGS TO DO RIGHT NOW TO BE HAPPIER

If you're already in the workforce and you find yourself in a job that simply doesn't work for you or you're frustrated to be unemployed, don't despair. It will get better.

Now, I'd love to tell you to Slack your manager right now to tell them that you're out and never look back, but

- you'd never do something like that, not in a million years, and
- we're still living in a world where it's easier to find a new job when you're already employed.

Here's my advice for bolstering your distress tolerance in the meantime.

### *Sublimate*

Okay, so those jerks at work don't appreciate you. Well, instead of stewing and getting more and more upset and becoming a supervillain, use your powers for good. Does your nephew's Scout group need a leader who can show them how to tie knots the *right* way? Does your favorite nonprofit need some help with their website? What about the friend who's getting married? Can you channel your gifts into making three hundred overly fussy party favors for the place settings?

You'll feel better knowing your talents are not wasted; plus you'll get the appreciation you deserve.

## Meditate

This is hard for Productive people because you're not naturally inclined to be still and breathe, but it will help, I promise. I suggest starting with sound baths—you can find great ones online—as the easiest way to get into a space you might not be familiar with.

Then guided meditation can help you reset your overburdened brain. Before you know it, the things that bothered you about the ham-fisted klutzes you work with will barely register for you. Just kidding. You'll never stop noticing their flaws, but you will be less bothered by them.

## Practice grounding techniques at work

What if I told you, you can smile and nod and be your congenial self *and* channel all the rage and sadness you feel? Well, you can. Grounding techniques, like envisioning all your negative energy draining from the top of your head down into the floor beneath your dress shoes, really work. I find visualizations like that to be the most effective, but you can also try breathing techniques. Square breathing, also called box breathing, can help calm you down and find peace in chaos. Inhale for four counts, hold for four counts, exhale for four counts, and hold for four counts. Repeat as long as it takes for the urge to burn it all down to subside.

*Build the best darn résumé and portfolio
the world's ever seen and start applying*

This is right in your wheelhouse. Just don't overthink it. While you're waiting for the perfect three-hour block to craft your cover letter, someone speedier scooped up the job three weeks ago.

Have your résumé ready to go when the perfect job—and now you know what it looks like—comes up.

## BET ON YOURSELF

At this point you know yourself and the factors that will make you happy at work. Patience isn't your strong suit; *you* are you're strong suit. You have everything you need to start finding something better and become a happier, more contented person.

Take it from the queen of being productive, Martha Stewart:

"So the pie isn't perfect? Cut it into wedges, stay in control, and never panic."

## TAKEAWAYS

- You value order, independence, and precision, but lots of people don't. Don't waste your time trying to fit in where you're not appreciated.
- Your ideal job has exacting standards, personal accountability, and lots of independence. You'll also be happy if your direct approach to communication is appreciated and understood there.
- Even when you're not in the perfect place, you can always find a way to use your gifts for good.

# CHAPTER 15

# THE PURPOSE-DRIVEN AT WORK

I think pride kills. Pride kills relationships, and pride kills businesses. . . . At some stage, you've got to be humble enough to step aside.

—Kim Tan

As far as service goes, it can take the form of a million things. To do service, you don't have to be a doctor working in the slums for free or become a social worker. Your position in life and what you do doesn't matter as much as how you do what you do.

—Elisabeth Kübler-Ross

Y ou can lead a rich, full life without achieving self-actualization. But you can make a much bigger impact if you have. If your strongest trait is Purpose-Driven, you might be on your way to, or already arrived at, self-actualization. Now, I'm not saying there's one type in this book that's happier when they're in the right job, but the Purpose-Driven are pretty darn happy. You might be Purpose-Driven dominant if:

- You're an Enneagram type 2 or 4, as are 17 and 16 percent of the Purpose-Driven, respectively.
- You're a high i on the DiSC assessment, as are 39 percent of your peers.
- You don't begrudge anyone your time if it's to serve a greater good.
- You know all kinds of people from various walks of life.
- Your next strongest Vander Index areas are Productive and Authentic, with 37 and 29 percent reporting strength in these.
- Anticipator is your weakest Vander Index area, with just 9 percent excelling there.
- You started or ran any number of social justice–related clubs in high school.
- You were voted most likely to win the Nobel Peace Prize.
- You loved history in school.
- Empathy is easy for you.
- Your enthusiasm for helping has been described as contagious.
- The world's problems are very apparent to you, but instead of being overwhelmed, you're inspired by them.

## MICRO TRAITS OF THE PURPOSE-DRIVEN

Looking closer at what it means to be Purpose-Driven, we've seen strong trends among our Unicorns. The happiest Purpose-Driven people we've met share three micro traits:

- **Selflessness.** Unsurprisingly, most Purpose-Driven people who love their jobs and thrive in them share a sense of selflessness. Says Beverly S., a school director, "When I was sixty years old, I sensed a strong calling to found a classical school in Houston for underserved children. My previous involvement in education was centered more on providing for my own children, but my current efforts are on behalf of underprivileged children who would otherwise not have the opportunity. Working in a low-income area of my city has been rewarding and fulfilling and has brought me great joy."

- **Focus on greater good.** The majority of the Purpose-Driven are concerned with doing the most good for the most people. Says nonprofit director Dave U., "Initially, I just loved being busy, getting involved in all sorts of activities, and love being seen and acknowledged. But then I learned that fulfilling a goal or objective that is most beneficial to all gives greater joy."

- **Resilience.** Being a successful and happy Purpose-Driven person at work requires backbone. You're not always going to win the first time around. Kelly O., a lawyer, credits resilience with her success: "I have succeeded in my areas of serving hurting humanity because I'm resilient. I'm inspired to win and am passionate about it, but I couldn't remain Purpose-Driven without resilience."

  Finance manager Joan K. agrees, saying resilience helps her keep going: "I stick with the project until I find a solution. I've learned not to be afraid to ask questions. The worst that can happen, especially if I'm just making a phone call, is that I'm told no. But usually I get at least a tidbit of information to continue going forward. I don't stop until I can go no further."

## THE HAPPIEST PURPOSE-DRIVEN PERSON YOU KNOW: DR. KIM TAN

It's one thing to be successful. It's another to use your success for good. Unfortunately, our newsfeeds are filled with stories of men who have achieved great success and wealth in their lives but who do not appear to be interested in paying it forward. Or using their success and power for good. Or even being terribly charitable. Instead, we see these so-called titans of industry doubling down on wealth and power, apparently not satisfied with what they already have.

Kim Tan is a prime example, to me, of what it *should* look like. He's achieved great success in business and lives as comfortably as anyone could hope for. And yet, he's not asking for more. He's . . . content. He has enough, and he's content with it. This is how it should be. And yet, it's a revolutionary concept, especially to us Americans.

It's not often that a successful businessperson says, "I've got all I need, thanks. I'm good. Let's see what we can do for others." That type of mentality isn't exactly conducive to the work they do. Our driven and ambitious leaders are supposed to strive for higher profits, greater output, bigger margins, always. But Tan is Purpose-Driven. And so enough is actually enough.

But just because Tan has enough doesn't mean he doesn't want more for the rest of us. He has an entrepreneur's spirit and a shepherd's heart. Tan wants to do his part to make the world a better place to live for the most vulnerable among us.

It all started when he and his family were visiting South Africa. They found themselves at a beautiful resort, but before that they first visited the largest slum outside Cape Town.

He immediately thought of writing a check to help the people in the slums. But that wasn't going to do much, he thought. That was when Tan became disillusioned with his own philanthropy.

"We do charity with good intentions and good hearts," he says. "But it can create a dependency culture. People lose the hustle, the motivation." If he really wanted to create lasting change for the people living in poverty, thought Tan, he'd need to build businesses that create jobs.

### Using the VC model for more than just profit

Tan describes himself as a "failed scientist," but says, "I'm kind of glad I failed. Failure is not a bad thing. It's what you do with it that matters."

Born in Malaysia and educated in England, he first set out to be an academic. He has a PhD in biochemistry and three postdoctoral fellowships.

"But then," he says, he "bailed" and built a number of biotech companies. Tan is humble, as is abundantly clear, so one has to dig a little bit to find that he invented sheep monoclonal antibodies and developed the first rapid tests for salmonella in chickens and for the atrazine pesticide in drinking water.

He says he was a lousy CEO. "I was a butterfly. I was interested in doing new things," he says. It was his experience as a founder of a biotech VC fund that helped inspire the solution to the question of poverty in South Africa.

Tan called the solution "social venture capital."

"Twentysomething years ago, there was no terminology for it," he says. "Now we call it impact investing."

Tan wanted to create employment and sustainable business for the people living in poverty. He saw potential for a game park resort and nature reserve and started investing in a region with more than 70 percent unemployment. His efforts became the Kuzuko Game Reserve, restoring forty thousand acres of degraded farmland and reintroducing the Big Five game animals to the area for the first time in 150 years. In recent years, they have planted thirty million spekboom plants on twelve thousand acres of land. The enterprise has created hundreds of jobs for the community and continues to be one of the largest employers in the district.

"When you create these kinds of jobs, it confers dignity on people," he explains. "And when a person has that sense of dignity, it's transformative."

Tan created a business network, the Transformational Business Network, made up of, as he calls them, disillusioned philanthropists and repentant bankers, lawyers, and accountants. Together, they have invested in numerous projects that benefit people and the world. The idea is to take the VC model and apply it to social and environmental issues. "It's a more disciplined approach," says Tan. "Businesses fail not because they were a bad idea but because they are undercapitalized and run out of cash. There is lots of crashing and burning amongst social enterprises."

Tan and his team seek out companies and founders who have solutions to social problems. "We ask them how much money they need and for how long. If we believe in them, we will make sure they have enough fuel in their tank to have liftoff."

**Developing people. And countries.**

While the difference Tan's work makes on an individual level is what makes it so rewarding, it takes thinking big to get there.

"For countries to develop, they need to move from the informal microbusinesses to the formal small- and medium-sized enterprise [SME] sector of the economy," he says. "People need to work; they need to have rights and access to health care and pensions."

And, crucially, Tan explains, these workers need to become taxpayers. The tax base of developing countries is very narrow, so governments don't have enough money to do things like fix roads, build schools, or provide other services for their citizens.

Other endeavors supported by Tan and his colleagues include forty-two computer training centers in South Africa, a prison call center in Singapore that has helped reduce recidivism rates to less than 6 percent, and a chain of five thousand low-cost schools, charging around five dollars a month, in six countries with two million pupils.

Tan says that it's meeting former prisoners who are now gainfully employed or talking to a woman who rose from life as a low-paid maid to become a trainer at one of the computer centers that makes his work so meaningful.

"We have loads and loads of these kinds of stories," he says.

**Contentment is key**

Tan is a walking example of how much purpose matters. "All companies have purpose," he says, "but is it meaningful?"

For those young people who would follow in Tan's path, he recommends getting good work experience first. "You will realize how competitive the world is, and only then will you become useful to us," he says, laughing. Above all, he says, "Don't do it on your own. Find other fools to do it together. All the things I've done, it's because I've had really good people—smart, passionate people—around me."

Tan reminds us, too, that, "contentment and gratitude are really good virtues." And happiness and contentment go hand in hand. What Tan has found for himself is what he wishes to provide to everyone working within his Transformational Business Network.

"We need to be creating environments for human flourishing," he says. "We were created in a garden. We need to be in places of beauty. Slums are not good places for human flourishing. Offices, factories, and churches should be but often are not. We need to create these environments."

Whether it's literally creating a flourishing environment in the form of game reserves that prevent deforestation or helping humans get the training they need to create their own places of beauty, Tan's purpose is to help us all find contentment.

## WHAT HAPPINESS AT WORK LOOKS LIKE FOR YOU IF YOU'RE PURPOSE-DRIVEN

If you have any Purpose-Driven tendencies at all, meaningful work is essential to you. And the straighter and shorter the line you can draw between your work and tangible positive impact, the better. When you're Purpose-Driven, you need a problem to solve, the freedom to take action, and a team to work with and benefit from your efforts.

As a Purpose-Driven person, you likely find tremendous joy in serving others and fulfillment in working toward something bigger than you. You tend to be bolder in asking for what you need to advance your mission, and you are wise enough to know your strengths and weaknesses.

The important difference between someone who is Purpose-Driven and what can better be described as a "merry martyr" is that the happiest Purpose-Driven people have figured out how to give to others, a cause, or another calling without losing themselves. If you can continuously pour from a full cup and you find yourself renewed in the work and not depleted by it, you're a Purpose-Driven person who's figured it out.

## THE JOB FOR YOU

In our survey, the happiest Purpose-Driven people have jobs where they're in a position to help people. This is not surprising, but what is interesting is that a Purpose-Driven person's happy place appears to be industry agnostic. We have representatives in business and finance, health, government, legal, the church, and, of course, nonprofits.

Careers where the Purpose-Driven thrive:

- Guidance counselor
- Lawyer / public defender
- Government official
- Physical therapist
- Server
- Nonprofit director
- Social worker
- Financial planner
- Personal trainer
- Beautician
- Nurse
- Funeral director
- Human resources manager
- Chaplain
- Teacher

Purpose-Driven people can thrive anywhere, but the same six workplace happiness factors apply to them as with all types.

*Having a good boss*

As a Purpose-Driven person, it's likely you will eventually be the leader, but until then you need a boss who is as mission driven as you are.

"Part of the reason I love my job is that I serve with leaders who love what they do. Our senior leadership manages our team incredibly effectively," says campus pastor Isaac D.

"My boss is always there to help and support me making genuine connections with students and helping others," says career adviser Genna H.

Jim C., who works for the government, says his boss helps him succeed by explaining the why of tasks rather than just telling him what to do. He says, "If I know the reason for the task I'm performing and what the end result needs to be, I will work harder than anyone to get the job done efficiently. My boss knows this and fills me in accordingly."

*Work-life balance*

Some Purpose-Driven professions lend themselves better than others to work-life balance, but for many, it's okay if the lines are blurred.

"I love that I can't take my work home with me," says hairstylist Kendall K. "It enables me to give it my all when I've got clients in the chair but then tune out when I go home."

Randal G., on the other hand, doesn't mind taking his work home with him. "Working for the state, especially in my position, doesn't really have an off switch. It's great, though, because I'm helping people. Plus, this job is a privilege I know I won't always have."

For attorney Jordan F., having her priorities straight is key to happiness in work and in life. She says, "As a new mom trying to balance a demanding career, I struggled with the feeling that I was constantly disappointing everyone (and of course still struggle with that sometimes). However, I started trying to focus on living my daily life in order of priorities: my faith, my family, my career. I can attest that putting my career last in that list has not made me an unreliable or unproductive employee; I believe the opposite is true (and believe my superiors would agree, as I am now a partner attorney). I know what my primary purposes are, and that has made me more sure in my roles, more productive with my work time, and (I believe) led to less regret. In many ways my job helps me improve and fulfill my purpose in those higher priority roles—and I believe that satisfaction and purpose fulfillment has a lot to do with my dedication and success in the workplace."

## Making enough money

Purpose-Driven people are happy when they're doing what they love and getting paid well for it, but money doesn't matter as much as the mission.

"I mean, I would do it for free if I could," says Kayleigh I., a makeup artist. "I love being able to help people feel great about themselves. But getting paid is better."

"Teaching people how to strengthen and care for their body is very rewarding," says physical therapist Josh J. "And it's a career that is in demand, so the pay is good."

Being Purpose-Driven helps Melissa M., an executive director at a foundation, feel content with less money. She says, "Knowing my purpose is what gets me out of bed to do what I am called to do. It's what makes hard days easier to handle, and problems feel less weighty. The moment I forget my purpose, running a whole organization feels daunting and overwhelming. Raising millions of dollars feels impossible, and other, higher paying jobs start to look more appealing. The anecdote to discouragement is being Purpose-Driven. I can motivate my team, encourage my donors, and inspire my volunteers with this single attribute. It's the quality I can't afford to lose."

## *Autonomy and flexibility*

The Purpose-Driven like solving problems, but they don't always like solving the same problems over and over. In that case, they need autonomy and flexibility to explore different topics.

Becca C. says that's why she loves being a lawyer: "My work is characterized by its variety. Each case is unique and involves different stories and circumstances. Whether in civil, criminal, or nonlitigation matters, lawyers have access to a wide variety of problems and solutions. This diversity means that I'm never bored, and each case is a new challenge and an opportunity to learn."

Knowing that he was personally responsible for people helped Don D. find meaning in his career: "I am retired from the aerospace industry. While working there, I always knew I had other people's lives in my hands based on the quality of the work I did."

## *Professional growth*

Purpose-Driven people like learning, but only if it's directly related to the good they can do for others.

"My least favorite thing about my job is the seemingly constant need to be trained up on new systems. I didn't go to school for data entry or software development. It's so frustrating," says social worker Tom M.

## Meaningful work

If you're Purpose-Driven, one of your favorite things is seeing the results of your efforts. Satisfaction that comes with "being part of something bigger" is all well and good, but often Purpose-Driven people prefer more concrete evidence of how the work they do benefits the world around them.

"I feel my work has purpose, it aligns with my personal values and goals, I love my coworkers, and I love seeing people's lives change," says Jessica W., a program director for a nonprofit.

"Making a difference in people's lives and sharing tools that help people live more joyfully and more authentically—that's what I love most about my job," says Suzanne M., a counselor.

---

"Mankind was my business.
The common welfare was my business;
charity, mercy, forbearance, and
benevolence, were all my business.
The dealings of my trade were but a
drop of water in the comprehensive
ocean of my business!"

---

## WHERE THE PURPOSE-DRIVEN
## MIGHT STRUGGLE

We've found Purpose-Driven people are determined doers, but even they can lose steam in their quest to make the world a better place. Red tape, not feeling like their work has meaning or working toward something they don't believe in, being asked to do too much, and the sadness that they so often encounter in their line of work can all lead to burnout and unhappiness in their jobs.

### The bureaucracy of it all

No one *likes* paperwork (okay, except maybe our friends the Prepared), but Purpose-Driven people get really frustrated with it.

"In an organization like ours," says campus pastor Isaac G., "there is bureaucracy and systems and processes that may be a little cumbersome."

Senior manager of HR and guest services Bobbie K. sums up the part of her job she doesn't like in one word: "Paperwork."

### Values not aligning

If you feel like you're working against what you believe your purpose is, it's time to leave. Debra H. says, "I worked twenty-five years in corporate America. In the last five years of that job, I felt like I was adding to the degradation of society by going to work. My values and the values of the company did not align any longer. I could not continue working for the company. Instead, I wanted to have purpose, meaning, and intentionality in my daily work. In 2018, I moved to Colorado from Iowa. Shortly after, I left my corporate job and started my own business as a leadership consultant."

## *Toiling hard while the grasshopper sings*

Frustration for Purpose-Driven people can grow to resentment pretty quickly if they see colleagues not working as diligently as they do.

"We are very slow to fire anyone, so there are a couple of employees who are kind of just hanging on that probably should be let go," says Ron M., who works in local government.

"I'm fine being asked to go above and beyond, and I'd be happy to do it," says nursing home caregiver Janie F. "But when I'm killing myself to get things done and wear ten different hats while my colleagues seem completely disengaged, it's really upsetting."

"Personality conflicts within my team or on other teams are the hardest to deal with," says nonprofit development director Jane P.

## *Sadness*

The Purpose-Driven are much more likely to go into fields where the stakes are higher. With the reward of helping people as spiritually and materially as Purpose-Driven people do comes the risk of witnessing a lot of tragedy.

Hospital chaplain Jerry P. says, "It's the sadness that I see during my job that makes it difficult, but being there for people's most vulnerable moments is a privilege. That being said, it's not always easy to let go of the terrible things you see."

Theologian Charity A. agrees that the work can be heavy: "Sometimes it makes you feel like you're carrying the burden of many people."

## THE HAPPY-AT-WORK CHECKLIST

As the poem goes, "Some kind of help is the kind of help that helping's all about, but some kind of help is the kind of help we all can do without." If you manage a Purpose-Driven person, make sure you're doing the following to achieve workplace happiness for you and them. If you *are* a purpose-driven person, let your team know which of the items below resonate with you.

**Help them see the purpose of what they're doing.** And help them see how their efforts contribute to the greater good.

**Let them be a part of the solution.** For some of our types, you need to figure out the plan before you invite them to be a part of it. But Purpose-Driven people thrive when they're invited to be a part of the solution. Trust them, give them clarity on how they can contribute, and let them see the effect of their work.

**Let them be in helping roles.** If you need someone to help train a new employee, if you need a project leader, if you need someone to pick up the food order from the front desk, this is the person to ask. Show them the meaning of the work and release them to do it.

**Help them advocate for themselves and treat them fairly.** In other words, don't take advantage of them.

Purpose-Driven people look at the full picture of a situation and decide what's best for the whole before they decide what's best for themselves. Make sure you have their backs and are advocating well for them for things like merit-based raises and promotions.

**Tell them when they're doing a good job.** Positive affirmation matters so much to the Purpose-Driven—it helps them see how the work they're doing matters. When it's genuine and deserved, make sure to be an encourager.

**Cut the red tape for them.** If you know about potential hold-ups or issues that a Purpose-Driven person may encounter in a project or task, let them know early on and help them figure out solutions around those things. They will be less likely to get frustrated with the red tape if it is not a surprise and they're able to take it into account when planning.

**Watch for any signs of comparison.** If your Purpose-Driven person is comparing themselves to others on the team or in the organization, that is the first sign that they're heading toward dissatisfaction and resentment.

**Help them process the emotions behind the role they've taken on.** Acknowledge that what they carry can be heavy sometimes. If you aren't equipped to walk that path with your Purpose-Driven person, provide them resources like free mental health coverage or other support.

**Check on them as a whole person.** Don't just ask how their projects or work is going. Ask—and genuinely care—about their life, their family, their vacation, their pets, or their hobbies outside of work. Purpose-Driven people need to know you see them fully, especially since they are doing the same for everyone around them.

## JOBS THAT DO NOT WORK FOR THE PURPOSE-DRIVEN

Everyone has a different tolerance for the so-called soul-crushing jobs, but as you might guess, the Purpose-Driven are the least equipped to handle them. Avoid at all costs:

- Most health insurance jobs
- Corrections officer
- State or national politics
- Sales
- Corporate law
- Advertising
- Finance
- Telemarketing
- Dickensian money lending

## THINGS A PURPOSE-DRIVEN PERSON CAN DO RIGHT NOW TO BE HAPPIER

Already working and hating it? Looking for a job yet remain frustratingly unemployed? You can make it better even before you land your dream job.

Here's my advice for Purpose-Driven people who are currently miserable.

### Help others in another capacity

You like helping people and seeing the results of your efforts. If you can't get paid to do that, go find a way to do it for free. There are plenty of opportunities for a sensitive, social soul like you. And not just the usual ones, either. You can find the big, important projects your heart calls for. Consider volunteering as a hospice volunteer to keep vigil for the dying, gear up and head toward natural disasters as everyone else is fleeing, describe the new fall fashions to the blind (maybe not that last one).

Irish novelist Marian Keyes was at a low point in her life when she suddenly decided to bake a friend a cake. When she couldn't be interested in anything else about life, she baked. And she baked and baked, delivering baked goods to everyone she knew, until she eventually felt better. You can read all about it and get recipes from her book *Saved by Cake*.

### Be patient

If you're frustrated that the work you're doing doesn't seem to be paying off, try to take a step back. Change doesn't happen overnight, and you can't solve all the world's problems yourself. Give yourself some grace, and give the universe a chance to catch up with you. While you wait, watch some inspirational movies like *Invictus*, *Miracle*, or *Hidden Figures*.

### Find inspiration in the animal world

Let's be honest: People can be incredibly disappointing. You might need to take yourself out of the human world for a bit and find solace with animals. I had a friend who got through some tough times by watching elephants on the elephant cams at the San Diego Zoo Safari Park. Start following Moo Deng on social media, find some nature documentaries (the ones geared toward children—no one wants to see a baby seal getting eaten by a polar bear when they're not at their best), or go walk some dogs at the humane society. People can be terrible to each other. Animals tend to be more civilized.

## KEEP THE FAITH

At this point, you know yourself and the factors that will make you happy at work. You're a good person with the ambition to do good for the world. You just have to find the right place to go. Luckily, that can be almost anywhere, and, says Plato, "Happiness springs from doing good and helping others." Keep being you and you'll be happy in no time.

## TAKEAWAYS

- You are sensitive and outgoing; your ideal job will utilize both of these characteristics.

- Your ideal job is one where your work directly benefits people, the planet, or animals.
- You are made of sterner stuff and can handle life's most challenging moments.

# CONCLUSION

You deserve to be happy. You deserve a job you love and a life that fulfills you.

Life is short, precious, and fragile. This hard truth has cruelly confronted me and my family during the writing of this book. But if any good can come of a diagnosis you never want to get, it's that it can be a wake-up call to stop doing what doesn't serve you and to start doing what your heart and brain implore you to do.

I think of legends like the late "Crocodile Hunter," Steve Irwin, who loved his job so much it was infectious. People who never cared about conservation, were terrified of sharks and snakes, or had no interest in visiting Australia were swept up in his passion for animals. He would tell his viewers, "My job, my mission, the reason I've been put onto this planet, is to save wildlife. And I thank you for comin' with me."

Thank *you* for coming with me as we've embarked on another mission: discerning your path to happiness at work. We can learn a lot from others, famous and otherwise, who love their jobs and who hate their jobs. But the biggest takeaway here is this: The most important person to learn from is yourself. When you know who you are—truly what makes you you—you can begin to narrow your wide ocean of options and draw that much closer to finding the work you are wired to do.

# NOTES

*one*

1. Jim Harter, "3 Key Insights into the Global Workplace," Gallup, June 12, 2024, https://www.gallup.com/workplace/645416/key -insights-global-workplace.aspx.

2. Luona Lin, Juliana Menasce Horowitz, and Richard Fry, "Most Americans Feel Good About Their Job Security but Not Their Pay," Pew Research Center, December 10, 2024, https://www.pewresearch .org/social-trends/2024/12/10/job-satisfaction/.

*two*

1. World Happiness Report 2024, https://worldhappiness.report/.

2. Evgenia I. Lysova, Luke Fletcher, and Sabrine El Baroudi, "What Makes Work Meaningful?" *Harvard Business Review*, July 12, 2023, https://hbr .org/2023/07/what-makes-work-meaningful.

3. Kim Parker and Juliana Menasce Horowitz, "Majority of Workers Who Quit a Job in 2021 Cite Low Pay, No Opportunities for Advancement, Feeling Disrespected," Pew Research Center, March 9, 2022, https:// www.pewresearch.org/short-reads/2022/03/09/majority-of-workers -who-quit-a-job-in-2021-cite-low-pay-no-opportunities-for-advancement -feeling-disrespected/.

4. Matthew A. Killingsworth, Daniel Kahneman, and Barbara Mellers, "Income and Emotional Well-Being: A Conflict Resolved," *Proceedings of the National Academy of Science* 120, no. 10 (March 2023), https:// pubmed.ncbi.nlm.nih.gov/36857342/.

## *four*

1. Jennifer D. Nahrgang, Hudson Sessions, Manuel Vaulont, and Amy Bartels, "Make Your Side Hustle Work," *Harvard Business Review*, March 18, 2020, https://hbr.org/2020/03/make-your-side-hustle-work.

2. "Meditation: A Simple, Fast Way to Reduce Stress," Mayo Clinic, n.d., https://www.mayoclinic.org/tests-procedures/meditation/in-depth/meditation/art-20045858.

3. Morgan Kelly, "Sowing Seeds of Happiness: Emotional Well-Being While Home Gardening Similar to Other Popular Activities, Study Finds," High Meadows Environmental Institute, May 10, 2020, https://environment.princeton.edu/news/emotional-well-being-while-home-gardening-similar-to-other-popular-activities-study-finds/.

4. Not just a great movie name, "cool runnings" means "peace be the journey."

## *seven*

1. Amiee Ball, "Overcoming the Dark Side of Being a Problem-Solver," *Forbes*, May 8, 2023, https://www.forbes.com/councils/forbesbusinesscouncil/2023/05/08/overcoming-the-dark-side-of-being-a-problem-solver/.

## *eight*

1. Sarah Youngblood Gregory, "The Mental Health Benefits of Nature: Spending Time Outdoors to Refresh Your Mind," Mayo Clinic Press, March 4, 2024, https://mcpress.mayoclinic.org/mental-health/the-mental-health-benefits-of-nature-spending-time-outdoors-to-refresh-your-mind/.

## *nine*

1. This is a quote from *The Caucasian Chalk Circle*, a play by Bertolt Brecht. I came to the community theater production of it prepared to be underwhelmed, but was pleasantly surprised by how good it was.

## ten

1. Alex Hawgood, "Cole Escola's Broadway Sensation *Oh, Mary!* Started with a Funny Note to Self," *W*, July 25, 2024, https://www.wmagazine.com/culture/cole-escola-oh-mary-broadway-interview.

## twelve

1. "Only 5% of Employees Prefer Working in the Office," HRO Today, December 22, 2023, https://www.hrotoday.com/news/only-5-of-employees-prefer-working-in-the-office/.

## thirteen

1. Jack Kelly, "The Role of the Personality Hire Who Brings the Workplace 'Vibes,'" *Forbes*, December 18, 2023, https://www.forbes.com/sites/jackkelly/2023/12/18/the-role-of-the-personality-hire-who-brings-the-workplace-vibes/.

# ACKNOWLEDGMENTS

I will be forever indebted to my wife, Adrienne, for this work. She has been the true compliment to any gifts I have. But long before now, she saw in me a wiring that led to starting the company we have run for the last seventeen years. Without her vision and guidance, I doubt I could have found work that matches my wiring so well.

Additionally, I want to thank every previous employer I have worked for over the years. I advise candidates all the time to "look for the job that you could never do today if you hadn't had all the jobs you had up until today." Without all of the experiences that led up until now, I couldn't do what I get to do now. Thank you for your patience and the experience you gave me that has led me to work I truly love.

I am not sure how to adequately thank my colleague Elizabeth Paulson for her tireless work on this project. She has been the tip of the spear in bringing this research and writing together, and is the embodiment of a benediction.

Finally, thanks to all of those who have supported me and this work. The team at HarperCollins has been amazing to work with. Thanks to Tim Burgard and Josh deLacy and all of the others at HC. Thanks to my agent, Esther Fedorkevich, for her guidance and representation. And thanks to Warren Bird for helping gather expert surveys and giving our research the level of excellence that is so hard to find.

# INDEX

jobs that do not work
  for Agile Unicorns, 76–77
  for Anticipator Unicorns, 120–21
  for Authentic Unicorns, 59
  for Connected Unicorns, 192–93
  for Curious Unicorns, 175–76
  for Fast Unicorns, 40–41
  for Prepared Unicorns, 138
  for Productive Unicorns, 232–33
  for Purpose Driven Unicorns, 256
  for Self-Aware Unicorns, 157
  for Solver Unicorns, 100
  see also struggles
Jung, Carl, 43

Kahneman, Daniel, 13
Kamil, Susan, 222
Keyes, Marian, 247
Khong Tai, Sandra, 84–91
Killingsworth, Matthew A., 13
knowing yourself, 16. see also Authentic
  Unicorns
Kübler-Ross, Elisabeth, 237

Lasso, Ted, 43
learning
  to contribute to your happiness, 10
  by Curious Unicorns, 163
*Legally Blonde*, 8
Likable Unicorns, 195–213
  best jobs for, 203–4
  example of, 198–203
  happiness at work for, 203, 205–6
  happiness-improving techniques for,
    211–12
  managing, 209–11
  micro traits of, 196–98
  struggles for, 208–9
Lincoln, Abraham, 159

*Mad Men*, 1–2, 18
*Mamma Mia! Here We Go Again*, 105–6
management
  of Agile Unicorns, 75–76
  of Anticipator Unicorns, 118–20
  of Authentic Unicorns, 57–59

bad, 3
  of Connected Unicorns, 190–92
  of Curious Unicorns, 174–75
  of Fast Unicorns, 38–40
  of Likable Unicorns, 209–11
  of Prepared Unicorns, 135–37
  of Productive Unicorns, 229–32
  of Purpose Driven Unicorns, 254–56
  of Self-Aware Unicorns, 155–57
  of Solver Unicorns, 98–100
Massie, Robert, 220
meaningful work
  for Agile Unicorns, 73
  for Anticipator Unicorns, 116
  for Authentic Unicorns, 56
  for Connected Unicorns, 189
  for Curious Unicorns, 172–73
  for Fast Unicorns, 36–37
  and happiness at work, 12
  and *ikigai* concept, 15–16
  for Likable Unicorns, 207
  for Prepared Unicorns, 133
  for Productive Unicorns, 227–28
  for Purpose-Driven Unicorns, 251
  for Self-Aware Unicorns, 153
  for Solver Unicorns, 95–96
Mellers, Barbara, 13
memory, of Connected Unicorns, 181–82
meticulousness, of Prepared Unicorns, 125
micro traits
  of Agile Unicorns, 65
  of Anticipator Unicorns, 107
  of Authentic Unicorns, 44–45
  of Connected Unicorns, 181–82
  of Curious Unicorns, 162–63
  of Fast Unicorns, 26–27
  of Likable Unicorns, 196–98
  of Prepared Unicorns, 124–25
  of Productive Unicorns, 216–17
  of Purpose Driven Unicorns, 238–40
  of Self-Aware Unicorns, 143
  of Solver Unicorns, 83–84
Miralles, Francesc, 15
Mollett, Ross, 198–203
money, 3
  for Agile Unicorns, 72

# ABOUT THE AUTHOR

WILLIAM VANDERBLOEMEN, founder and CEO of Vanderbloemen Search Group, is a renowned speaker, author, and expert on leadership, workplace culture, and staffing issues. In 2008, William pioneered a brand-new industry: executive search for faith-based organizations. What started on a card table has grown into a globally recognized leader in talent. A firm believer in data, William has discovered trends and traits common to the best and happiest leaders through more than three thousand executive searches and thirty thousand interviews. He is the bestselling author of *Be the Unicorn: 12 Data-Driven Habits that Separate the Best Leaders from the Rest.*